Chesapeake Bay
AND TIDEWATER

COVE POINT

OLD LIGHTHOUSE . . . In 1828 this light began sending out its beam from Cove Point, at the mouth of the Patuxent River. It still does so, and is one of the oldest lighthouses on the Bay. By telescope, the keeper used to identify all inbound freighters and report their imminent arrival to Baltimore.

Chesapeake Bay
AND TIDEWATER

A · AUBREY BODINE

Honorary Fellow of the Photographic Society of America
Fellow of the National Press Photographers

Bonanza Books
New York

WHEN THE WIND BLOWS

This edition is published by Bonanza Books,
a division of Crown Publishers, Inc.
by arrangement with Bodine & Associates, Inc.
a b c d e f g h
BONANZA 1980 EDITION

Manufactured in the United States of America

Library of Congress Cataloging in Publication Data

Bodine, A Aubrey, 1907–1970.
    Chesapeake Bay and Tidewater.

    Includes index.
    1. Chesapeake Bay—Description and travel—Views.
2. Maryland—Description and travel—1951–
—Views. 3. Virginia—Description and travel—
1951- —Views. 4. Delaware—Description and
travel— 1951- —Views. I. Title.
F187.C5B6 1980   917.55′18   79-24663
ISBN 0-517-30948-3

AN INTRODUCTION

THERE IS NOTHING NEW about an alert visitor's ability to see with appreciative eyes the beauties or oddities or grandeurs which a lifetime resident in any community has never more than noted. And perhaps, for that reason, there should be no surprise over a born mountaineer's discovery, in the Chesapeake Bay and its estuaries and the tidewater lands, such scenes as usually elude the people who all their lives have dwelt nearby, indifferent.

In the splendid pages which follow, it is safe to say, there are scores and scores of things which for decades have gone unnoticed by most of us—until an artist's eye has detected them at just the right time of day, in the right time of the year and in the right kind of weather, and in the flash of a camera-shutter has preserved each object for all time at its unique best. Aubrey Bodine has been doing that all his adult life, and thereby bringing astonishment and delight to countless people. Here is the evidence, in a collection to suit all tastes. Of the scenes many are so simple that they look as though "Anybody could make that picture." (Try it some day, when you have a lot of time and film). Others unmistakably call for great ingenuity in the selection of the exact viewpoint, the exact scope, the exact timing.

How greatly Aubrey Bodine excels most others in artistic judgment and insight as well as skill, in perseverance and patience as well as industry, nobody knows better than a newspaper editor on whose staff is a photographic genius. I was editing The Baltimore Sunday Sun years ago when a shy youth submitted some strikingly fine photographs for publication. He was then a novice in The Sun's commercial-art office, gnawing his knuckles in impatience over the dull daily business of making routine pictures of routine goods for routine sale. The young redhead was so eager to do creative work on the Sunday staff that he might almost have come for nothing at all. But he calmly stated that nobody could want him to provide good pictures at poor pay. His way of putting it startled the editors and almost made the business-manager blush (which is quite a feat) and he got the raise. Did Bodine then move to better quarters? Or eat oftener? Or add to his wardrobe? Or take an extra day off? Not a bit of it. He bought (with his own funds—still very small) one horribly expensive lens after another. When his thrifty editor declined to put some new device or other in the photographic laboratory, this extraordinary youth grandly bought the device himself and presented it to us. Early in the morning he could be found testing out some new paper; long after quitting time and on off-days he experimented in a new light for his printing. I dare not guess how many times, when a particular feature was scheduled for the current week, and Bodine had already made an illustration for it, we could not get it from him—*he* was not satisfied with the shot, and doggedly insisted on going back (perhaps to a distant county) when the light would be just right for the sort of picture he wished to submit. Nobody ever heard of his supplying a picture which was only pretty good; it had to be what he regarded as the best possible picture of the subject. That sort of experience is something of a strain on an editor in a hurry, but the wise editor learns in time not to try to buck fate.

OXEN, CALVERT COUNTY, MARYLAND

A good many years have passed since then. New editors have come and gone, but Bodine is eternal—I hope. He is as angular as in boyhood, and as redheaded, and as unyielding in the integrity which still prevents him from doing anything but his best. It seems to be a good policy, for not a year passes without his accumulating new awards in national and international photographic competitions, and rarely a week without at least one of his flawless recordings of some Maryland scene reproduced in The Sunday Sun. Recent years have witnessed a growing zeal for the preservation of our colonial homes and churches. No one can estimate how largely that happy result was stimulated by admiration for those ancient shrines and welcoming doorways as disclosed by a Bodine print. Some of the best of such prints were presented in his book, "The Face of Maryland," to which this present work is a sort of sea-going supplement, dealing with the shining surface of the great Bay and its tributaries, and the lovely shores within the adjacent states of Maryland and Delaware and Virginia.

In Tidewater the watercourses are many, and they are important. For a great many years after the 1634 settlement planters moved about by barge or sail instead of by road, because the water route often was both shorter and surer. Hence the manor houses themselves were placed in proximity to the rivers and creeks, so that to this day one rides by automobile for miles past some of the noblest old mansions without catching a glimpse of one of them. By motor-launch he sees them all. On page 32 you will find an aerial view of a tidal region which is a mere network of streams, with no highway at all, and while this is an extreme, it is a useful reminder of why the early settlers sensibly paid far more attention to water transport than to roads. You will find on page 15 a reminder of how greedy the tides of Chesapeake can be, sweeping away structures and even islands of considerable size, once thickly settled.

The geography of the Bay changes, then, as do the identities and the habits of the people on its shores. But a great deal goes on unchanged from generation to generation, and it is largely the things that change not, save to grow softer and more beautiful with age, that have captured Bodine's affectionate attention. The individual reader may be particularly fascinated by the patterns which the camera unexpectedly establishes, whether in the sparkling light and intense shadow of the water's surface about the ship's hull (page 138) or in the curious and multiplied repetition of the Washington Monument's noble theme in a distant and wholly unrelated bridge-railing (page 39). Or by the pictured elegy in a country churchyard (page 54) where a practiced eye can discern among the conventional monuments a time-worn millstone beneath which lies the ancient miller, forever close to his own familiar tool. Or in those wondrous pictures of the fishing-crews cruising out to the pounds or hauling in their picturesque nets, or of the crabbers at their labors. Or, like the writer, he may find that he can gaze spellbound at them all. Of the thousands and thousands of pictures Aubrey Bodine has made of the Bay and its tributaries, these pages seem to contain just about the best.

Mark S. Watson

DIGGES HOUSE, YORKTOWN, VIRGINIA

"GIVE ME LIBERTY, OR GIVE ME DEATH" . . . Patrick
Henry shouted those immortal words in this venerable
structure, St. John's Episcopal Church of Richmond, on
March 20, 1775, during the second Virginia Convention.
The central portion of the church was built in 1741, eight
years after Richmond was founded. In the churchyard are
the graves of George Wythe, first professor of law in the
United States, and Elizabeth Arnold Poe, actress-mother
of Edgar Allan Poe.

My Bay

WHEN I was selecting the photographs to be used in this book a friend remarked. "You've got 40 years of work here." In one respect he was right. As a photographer for the Baltimore Sunday Sun I have spent 40 years taking pictures of the Chesapeake Bay and its country. And yet in another respect my friend was wrong. I said to him: "When you come right down to it, this isn't the work of 40 years, but actually, of less than 80 seconds." Some of the pictures were made in just 1/1000 of a second. The longest ones, the time exposures, didn't take over 10 seconds. There are 252 pictures in the book. Only 4 of these are time exposures. The rest were made between one second and 1/1000 second. It comes to less than 80 seconds.

Of course when I figure this way I don't take into account any traveling time, planning time or darkroom work. Later on I'll tell you about some pictures that really took some time to make.

The first Chesapeake Bay picture I ever made was of the workboat races at Cambridge, Maryland, in 1929. I didn't include that one in the book, but I have made use of other early shots. And when I first began to make pictures on the Bay I used glass plate negatives.

The Digges House (page 7) recalls an early but pleasant assignment given me in 1929 by Mark S. Watson, at that time editor of the Sunday Sun, to make a series of pictures showing the restoration work done on this house by John Scarff, the Maryland architect. I left Baltimore aboard the *Yorktown* and I was literally tossed on the dock at Yorktown at 3 o'clock the next morning. My sole companion was an ice house watchman who kept me entertained until daybreak, when I started to work.

Probably the most enjoyable picture expedition I ever made was in 1939 on the four-masted *Doris Hamlin.* I boarded the schooner in Baltimore and it took us a week to reach Newport News because we were becalmed several times. I was completely out of touch with the world, leading the life of Reilly, and getting some wonderful pictures. It was on this trip that I made the picture of the *Edna Hoyt* (page 13). In 1940 the *Doris Hamlin,* carrying a crew of ten, sailed for the Canary Islands. She disappeared mysteriously and to this day nothing has been heard of her or the crew.

I have a picture of the last commercial sloop on the Bay, the *J. T. Leonard,* but unfortunately my files are without a good shot of a pungy. The pungies have all disappeared, yielding to more shallow-draft vessels, such as skipjacks. However, the name "pungy pink" still lingers in the Bay country. It describes the unique shade—a lovely and delicate pink—that adorned the hull of every pungy. To contrast with the pink, the rails of the pungy were painted a dark green—some called it watermelon green. The pink and green, combined with the white sails, made one of the loveliest color patterns I have ever seen on the Bay. I hope some day a fabric designer will use "pungy pink." It would be a sensation on a strawberry blonde.

Practically any part of the Chesapeake and its country has something of interest for the artist and the photographer, but in my estimation Horn Harbor, in Mathews County, Virginia, and Crisfield, Maryland, have more atmosphere than any other places. Horn Harbor (page 146) has an ancient, weathered air. I doubt if it has changed much in the last 100 years. There are no Neon lights, beer or Coke signs to scar or obscure the scenery. Horn Harbor is a fishing center and, consequently, it offers unlimited opportunities for scenes of drying nets, boats riding at anchor, fishermen, and action pictures around the packing house.

Crisfield (page 49) probably has even more color. I have been there many times, but I'm still intrigued with its streets and wharves, its crab pounds, and the activity on the isle of Jersey which lies off Main Street and once was connected to the town by a patchwork drawbridge. The lower section of Main Street reminds me of an old-time Western town. Many of the buildings have those second floor false fronts, most of them haven't been painted for years and a great many lean at odd angles. A young artist could settle down here and have material for the rest of his life.

Crisfield is the connecting point for the outside world with Tangier and Smith islands (page 48 and 85) which lie along the Maryland-Virginia line. These islands are undoubtedly the most picturesque ones in the Bay. The only way to visit them is by private boat, summer excursion boats or on the mail boats which leave Crisfield every week day. The 12-mile trip through Tangier Sound is lovely, but often rough. The well-kept houses and narrow pathways on the islands are pictures of beauty and contentment. Up until a few years ago the natives did not let visitors use cameras on the island. Now they are friendly with photographers. But they still have no use for game wardens. Those officials are about as welcome as a hurricane.

One of the most thrilling sights on the Bay is to watch the menhaden fishermen work their nets (page 148). The first time I accompanied a crew out of Reedville, Virginia, we had to wait ten hours before a school was sighted. As soon as it appeared two bunker boats, one manned by white men, the other by Negroes, went into action. And as soon as the crews began to haul the purse seines the air was filled with some wonderful chanting and singing. I know the books tell how the Negroes sing while they work. But this singing was done by the white crew. The Negroes didn't open their mouths.

Some of the pictures that appear in this book were made on the spur of the moment—and others took quite a bit of time. For example, "Dredging Over the Rocks," which appears on page 140, was snapped hurriedly and without any preparation. If the picture had not been made at that precise moment it wouldn't have been worth much. Some of the other pictures took much more time. The one of the Debtors' Prison in Accomac, Virginia (page 75) was made after five different visits. Each time the sun's axis was in the wrong position to brighten up the front. Finally on a lovely day I got what I wanted.

The picture of the tidewater mill (page 29) also required several trips. First I photographed it in a morning

light. Then I went back and made it in early afternoon. Still not satisfied, I tried it in early evening. I still didn't have what I wanted so I took one more picture—shortly after daybreak. That's the one that I used.

The picture of the Naval Academy midshipmen on parade (page 93) was the first such picture ever made and required a great deal of preparation. Arrangements had to be made for a Navy helicopter, clearance had to be obtained from various commands, and finally, the door of the helicopter had to be removed so I could get maneuverability with my camera. We hovered over Worden Field, the drillground at the Academy, while the companies marched on. After all 3600 midshipmen were lined up, nothing seemed to happen on the field. I had just made my first picture when the pilot started to leave the area, though I kept waving him to make another turn of the field. After we landed I found out that Admiral Turner Joy, USN, at that time superintendent of the Naval Academy, had ordered the helicopter away. It made so much noise that no commands could be heard on the field. I couldn't hear either for four days—until I got some hospital treatment. The weekly dress parade almost ended disastrously that day because of my picture. But I was forgiven when the admiral saw the picture. He asked for a large print for his office.

There are many strange sights to be seen in the Bay country if one gets away from the beaten track. The most unusual, until recent years, was to see yokes of oxen at work in Calvert County fields and woods—less than 25 miles from Washington, capital of the most machine-minded country in the world. Such a scene is pictured on page 6. Another unusual thing that caught my fancy was the oyster watcher (page 11). This man, who sits all day in a house out in Hampton Roads, has one of the world's most unusual occupations. He watches oyster beds to keep poachers away. And he really can't see what he is paid to watch!

On my trip to Smithfield, Virginia, I had visions of hams hanging from rafters in every store, signs on practically every corner advertising the glories of Smithfield ham, and field after field filled with peanut-fed hogs. I have yet to see any of these things. Instead I found a large, clean packing house which was the hub of the Smithfield ham business. To get a picture of this and the Pagan River (page 83) at the proper angle and elevation I mounted my camera on the porch of a large white house. I learned later that the house belonged to the Gwaltney family, the most famous name in Smithfield hams.

I included the picture of the Crisfield general store (page 62) because it is so typical of the tidewater store. The big food market is seldom seen in the Bay country. And the reason, I think, is because the people like to use their general store as a meeting house—to discuss politics, the weather and fishing. Incidentally, many strangers think that an unpainted house is the sign of poverty or laziness. That is not always correct. Many buildings, such as the Crisfield store, are made of virgin timber and need no paint.

The man pictured on page 86 was typical of the good

MASONIC TEMPLE, ALEXANDRIA, VIRGINIA

OYSTER WATCHER, HAMPTON ROADS, VIRGINIA

sturdy stock found throughout the tidewater country. The Virginia and Maryland watermen have the remarkable ability to steer without a compass, an almost uncanny ability to predict the weather without a barometer, and a certain unbelievable sixth sense to know when to stop a fishing boat over an area and announce, "This is where the fish is." If you want to have some fun with one of these watermen, tell him that you think it looks "calm." He will indirectly correct you by giving his opinion of the weather and pronouncing the word "calm" as "kam."

I have often been asked what is the most suitable time to photograph water scenes. My answer always is, early morning and late evening. In planning the picture used on the title page I surveyed the scene in the evening, planning my camera placement and what I wanted to *keep out* of the picture. The next morning I was up at 4 o'clock and I made the picture while the sun was rising. The sun rises rapidly and the difference of a minute or two is critical. At the time I felt that I had a good shot. What I made was judged the best pictorial news photograph of the year and it has won several other awards.

I am often asked how I find certain subjects. Some I get from reading old volumes—one of my hobbies is collecting books and material about the Bay country—but most of it comes from talking to people. I enjoy talking to people gathered in country stores, watermen standing around the wharves, country newspaper editors, county agents, and the like. They are wonderful people to know, and they know just about everything that's going on.

Sometimes I pick up a tip or a suggestion in a strange way. I was in Pittsburgh judging an international salon when a stranger suggested the use of a bridge railing as a pattern in a picture of the Washington Monument. The man couldn't remember the name of the bridge with the iron pickets but I decided the idea was good enough to investigate. At the first opportunity I drove over to Washington and searched until I found the bridge that gave me the picture which appears on page 39.

The Chesapeake Bay bridge photograph (page 34) was made at dusk. I purposely selected this time so I could make a ten second exposure to catch the car lights which would create a white streak, accentuating the curve of the bridge. I doubt very much if the picture can be duplicated from this angle and elevation. I made mine from the pilot house of the ferry boat *John M. Dennis*. The day after I made my shot the old Bay ferry left her berth near the bridge on her way to a new assignment on the west coast. Now there is nothing but pilings.

The picture that gave me the worst headache was the one of the superliner *United States* (page 134). When I decided to photograph the largest ship ever built in the Bay, in her native "habitat," she was thousands of miles away. So I had to wait until she returned to Hampton Roads for repairs. That wait took seven months. But I think the result was worth it.

Photographing the *United States* was a big thrill, but I always get a bigger thrill when I make a picture of a fleet of dredge boats moving over an oyster bed on a beautiful autumn day. That's a sight I hope I can keep photographing for the next 25 years.

A. AUBREY BODINE, *Hon. F.P.S.A., F.N.P.P.*
Baltimore, Maryland, January, 1967

11

FIRST LANDING . . . Lord Baltimore's colonists first landed at St. Clements Island—now called Blackiston—in the Potomac River, about 31 miles from its mouth. The cross commemorates the Mass said here by Father Andrew White, the first one in the Maryland colony.

GONE ARE THE DAYS . . . The *Anne Arundel* was one of many trim steamboats that once sailed out of Baltimore with passengers and freight for landings throughout the Bay country. The picture was made in 1936 at St. Marys City which was the capital of Maryland until 1694.

FIVE-MASTER . . . An era in Bay history ended in 1938 when the five-masted coasting schooner *Edna Hoyt* went out of service. She was one of only 58 such vessels ever built in this country and was the last to sail the Chesapeake. This photograph was made in 1936 in Baltimore harbor from the four-masted *Doris Hamlin*.

Bay of Yesterday

THE BAY was born of the ocean in a deep river valley a million or more years ago. Over vast ranges of time it has been bordered with jungle growth and jammed with ice floes and bergs. Mastodons, saber-toothed tigers and camels have roamed its country. Crocodiles and whales have played in its waters. Indians built their villages along the Bay tributaries at least 3,000 years ago.

Some believe that Thorfinn Karlsefni, a Viking, found the Bay while cruising along the Atlantic Coast in his dragon ship. That would have been in the Eleventh Century, nearly 500 years before Columbus sighted land. There is a possibility that John Cabot knew of the Bay in 1498. Many historians claim that the Spaniard Pedro Menéndez Marques was the true discoverer of the Bay. He reported its "many rivers and harbors" about 1573.

De Bry identified the Bay in his book in 1590. He called it Chesepiooc sinus, a name derived from the Indian words *Tschiswapeki* or *K'che-sepiack,* meaning highly salted body of standing water, or country on a great river.

Capt. John Smith searched the Bay in 1608 in his barge, with a crew of fourteen, including an herb doctor. He was the first to explore it in detail. After his findings were published, the Bay became a broad highway for the founders and would-be conquerors of the New World, for the valiant and the opportunists, who moved across the blue-green waters in a glittering pageant of history that rivals any pageant America has seen.

Much of America's early history was written along its shores. Jamestown was the first permanent English settlement in America. St. Marys City was the home of the Calvert Colonists and the capital of Maryland until 1694. Williamsburg was the capital of Virginia from 1699 to 1780, and one of the most important cities in the colonies. The Revolutionary War ended at Yorktown. The British were repulsed at Fort McHenry during the War of 1812, and during the battle Francis Scott Key was inspired to write the words to the "Star-Spangled Banner." The Bay also had a part in three other wars. During the War between the States it was a military highway for the North. During World Wars I and II, Liberty ships moved out carrying supplies for our armies. And in World War II the Navy's landing craft were tested on the Bay's beaches.

Much evidence of all this history still remains—on the battlefields, in the nation's shrines, in the old houses that dot the tidewater country, in the old ships rotting in the water. There is history too in the tidemill, in the Dutch windmill, and in the pictures of the old boats and other events that can no longer be seen on the Chesapeake.

THE BIG FREEZE . . . Normally the Chesapeake is free from ice, but occasionally a severe winter belies its location below the Mason-Dixon Line. This happened last in 1936. The Bay itself iced over completely for about 80 of its 195 miles—almost down to the Patuxent River. Its tributaries right on down to the James froze up. Fields of drift ice lay between the Virginia Capes. The dredge boats, framed by a necklace of icicles, sought shelter in Spa Creek, off Annapolis. They were immobilized for weeks. The icebreaker *Annapolis,* below, is attempting to smash its way through a crust of ice nine inches thick. In the distance is a line of ships held tight by the mass of ice.

LONG DOCK . . . Dogs huddle for warmth, foreground, against the penetrating chill of a foggy morning in the Baltimore harbor. The *City of Norfolk* is on the left. The *U.S.F. Constellation* is on the right.

SCOW SLOOP . . . These unusual craft were once common at the head of the Bay, and were used in areas where extreme shallow draft was necessary. The *Elsie*, below, was the last in service. She was abandoned about 1940.

VANISHING ISLAND . . . Once Holland Island, in Holland Strait, had a church, schoolhouse, thriving stores and a population of about 300. Around 1900, chunks of the island began to disappear in the Bay. Erosion became an increasing problem each year. By the 'Twenties families were forced to move. They tore down their houses, loaded the lumber on boats and sailed to the mainland where the houses were rebuilt. This house was one of the last on the island.

OUTLAWED . . . The use of sink boxes, which were anchored far out in the water to give duck hunters unexcelled shooting positions, was restricted by Federal regulations in the 'Twenties and prohibited during the 'Thirties as a conservation measure. For the same reason, swivel guns and "long-toms" have been outlawed.

THE AGE OF STEAM . . . This is one of the last double-header steam engine trains to cross the Pennsylvania Railroad's bridge over the Susquehanna River. Electric-powered engines are now used. In the distance can be seen the U. S. 40 toll span, and, beyond it, the bridge of the Baltimore & Ohio Railroad.

LONG DOCK . . . In the old days, before motor trucks began hauling produce from tidewater fields, Baltimore's famous Long Dock on Pratt Street was crowded all summer long with craft selling melons, tomatoes and potatoes. Note the hucksters' wagons pulling away with their loads of melons.

CANTON HOLLOW . . . This was a favorite anchorage for skipjacks, bugeyes, schooners and other Bay craft while they waited for dock space or cargo. They arrived with produce, carried away lumber, fertilizer or general cargo. The photograph looks north across the Baltimore harbor. It was taken over 40 years ago.

RIVALS . . . The *Potomac,* left, and the *Calvert* often raced after leaving Baltimore harbor. The *Potomac* served Rappahannock River points; the *Calvert* made landings on the Choptank and Tred Avon Rivers.

SHOWBOAT . . . This "floating theater" sailed up and down the Bay for 25 years. It had a seating capacity of about 500 (reserved seats cost 40 cents), and a repertoire that included such favorites as "Smilin' Through" and "Ten Nights in a Barroom." Edna Ferber spent a summer aboard soaking up background for her famous novel, "Show Boat."

OLD SHIPYARDS . . . All manner of sailing ships—rams, schooners, brigs, brigantines—were repaired in three shipyards that once sprawled along Key Highway at the foot of Federal Hill in Baltimore's inner harbor. The four-masted schooner, *Albert F. Paul,* is in the yards of Booz Brothers, Inc., which traced its origin back to 1849, days when Baltimore Clippers were still plying the sea lanes. The *W. P. Ward,* a two-masted schooner, is in the yards of Redman-Vane. The two yards—plus the Baltimore Ship Repair Company, which does not appear in the picture—were acquired by the United States Navy in 1942 and were razed to make way for additional repair yards used by the Bethlehem Steel Company's ship building division. Here many allied warships and cargo vessels, damaged by enemy action, were repaired during World War II. This photograph was made about 1932.

INVASION . . . Many of the men who fought in the invasions of Africa and the Southwest Pacific islands learned about amphibious operations on the sand beaches of Chesapeake Bay. For several years such quiet and remote places as Cove Point and Drum Point resounded to the noises of mock battle as blunt-nosed LCI's and LST's practised disgorging troops and tanks. Operations were conducted from three bases, Little Creek and Camp Bradford, near Norfolk, and the United States Operational Development Center, Atlantic, on Solomons Island, an elbow-like spit of land on the Patuxent River which is one of the most famous sport fishing centers on the Bay. This photograph, taken in November, 1943, at Solomons, was one of the first ever made of the strange-looking craft in action. LST's are shown landing right in the front yard of a deserted summer cottage.

OLDEST WARSHIP AFLOAT . . . *U.S.F. Constellation*, 38-gun frigate launched in 1794 in David Stodder's shipyard on Harris Creek. Nicknamed the "Yankee Race Horse," she was active through World War II when she served as a flagship for the Atlantic Fleet. Later it was refitted through donations and was destined to be moved to a permanent berth in Baltimore's Inner Harbor.

"OLD IRONSIDES" . . . Thousands of people lined Recreation Pier when the *Constitution* visited Baltimore in 1931. The frigate is now in the Boston Navy Yard. Her sister ship is pictured above.

MARINERS' MUSEUM ... On the banks of the James River near Newport News is the Mariners' Museum, one of the world's finest maritime museums. It was founded in 1930 and is devoted "to the culture of the sea and its tributaries, its conquests by man, and its influence on civilization." Included in its displays is a great quantity of material relating to the Chesapeake Bay.

"SMOKY JOE" ... The *Philadelphia,* better known as "Smoky Joe" because of the thick cloud of black smoke that trailed from her stack, plied between Baltimore and Love Point in all sorts of weather. She achieved a legendary reputation for her rescues and was immortalized in the ballad which began, "Ol' Cap'n Perry of the Love Point Ferry."

BALTIMORE'S OLDEST HOUSE . . . Mount Clare, built in 1754 by Dr. Charles Carroll, is the only colonial mansion left within the city of Baltimore and as such is the city's oldest house. In the eighteenth century its lawns swept almost to the bank of the Patapsco River which came close to what is now the Washington Boulevard. Mount Clare, surrounded by Carroll Park, is maintained as a museum.

CLAIMED BY THE BAY . . . The *Levin J. Marvel,* one of the last five rams to sail the Bay, sank off North Beach on August 12, 1955, with a loss of 14 lives. Rams, none of which is to be found on the Chesapeake today, are three-masted, bald-headed (without topmasts) and schooner-rigged. They were designed to carry heavy cargoes of lumber from the Carolina sounds. The first was built in Bethel, Delaware, in 1889.

MUSEUM . . . The Chesapeake Bay Maritime Museum, in St. Michaels, encompasses three buildings that serve as a repository of records and memorabilia of shipping and shipbuilding on the Bay. In the early nineteenth century, the boat yards of St. Michaels turned out many of the Clippers that made Baltimore a famous port.

WINDMILL . . . This was Maryland's last old windmill. It stood on the edge of the Honga River, and the Dutch-type mill dated back to about 1750.

WATER-LOGGED . . . When lumbermen were cutting large stands of pine from islands deep in the Eastern Shore marshes, log floats were a common sight on the creeks and rivers. This tow is bound for a community sawmill on the Honga River.

POINT LOOKOUT . . . The monument is in memory of some 3,000 Confederate prisoners who died in a Union prison camp that stood here. The name of each prisoner is lettered on the bronze tablets. This is on Point Lookout, the southern tip of Maryland's western shore, where the Potomac River meets the Bay. The point is one of four in the sailor's rhyme,

Point Lookout and Point Look-in,
Point-No-Point and Point Again.

Jamestown Island, Virginia

GLOUCESTER COURTHOUSE . . . This walled court square sits in the center of the seat of Virginia's Gloucester County. The courthouse, right, was erected in 1776, three years before the town was established. Next to it is the Debtors' Prison, built before 1750. The monument is in memory of the Confederate dead of Gloucester.

SINCE 1680 . . . Eastville, on the Eastern Shore of Virginia, has been a county seat since 1680. The old courthouse, center, was erected in 1731. To the left of it is Debtors' Prison, built in 1664 and said to be the oldest one in the country. In the "new courthouse" (not shown) are records dating back to 1632, the oldest continuous court records in America. Historians often consult them.

BIRTHPLACE OF THE NATION . . . The first permanent settlement in America by the English was made in 1607 on the island of Jamestown. And here, twelve years later, was set up the first representative government in the New World. Shown on the opposite page are the ruins of the eighteenth century Jacquelin-Ambler House. Seen through the window is the Jamestown National Monument.

HISTORY NOW . . . The Union ship *Hartford,* from which Adm. David Farragut issued his order "Damn the torpedoes! Go Ahead!" Allowed to rot at its anchorage, the fighting ship sank in the Elizabeth River in 1956. The aircraft carrier *Midway* is in the background.

SIDEWHEELER . . . This picture of the *Dorchester* was made in 1931 at Kinsale, Virginia. The sidewheeler was built especially for the Choptank-Tred Avon rivers run, and was later used for Washington service. She became known as the *Robert E. Lee,* and was dismantled in 1953.

TURNED BY THE TIDE . . . The last of the Bay country's "tide mills" as it appeared on an estuary of Mobjack Bay. The huge wooden wheel turned one way when the tide flowed in, the other way when it ebbed. No one knows just when the mill was built, but records indicate that it ground grain for Washington's army during the siege of Yorktown in the autumn of 1781.

DIVIDING LINE . . . Colonial Beach, Virginia, is a resort on the Potomac River. Piers such as this were built because bars and slot machines, illegal in Virginia, could be installed at the end—which technically is in Maryland.

PICNIC GROUNDS . . . Tolchester Beach, founded in 1877, long was popular with Baltimoreans. Millions journeyed to the Eastern Shore resort for picnics and church outings in steamers such as the *Louise* and the *Tolchester*.

OLD BAY LINE . . . The Baltimore Steam Packet Company, familiarly known as the Old Bay Line, was organized in 1840. Its ships plied between Norfolk and Washington and Norfolk and Baltimore until 1962. The *City of Norfolk,* above, was approaching Old Point Comfort, Virginia.

LAST FERRY . . . Until 1963, this ferry operated between Little Creek, near Norfolk, and Kipto-peke Beach, on the Eastern Shore of Virginia. It was the last one to offer regular service across the Chesapeake, and the pleasant trip usually took one hour and 25 minutes.

LAND OF THE BLACKWATER . . . This unusual photograph, which gives the curiously-shaped strips of land a primeval look, was made against the sun from an airplane flying over the Blackwater National Wildlife Refuge on the Eastern Shore of Maryland. The channel in the center is the Little Blackwater River. The convoluting shorelines formed by one small river illustrates why the Bay, which is fed by 48 principal tributaries, has a tidal shoreline of an estimated 5,100 miles, about 3,600 in Maryland and some 1,500 in the commonwealth of Virginia.

Bay Today

THE Chesapeake Bay is a fleet of skipjacks or a brace of log canoes riding the wind. It is an array of ocean-going vessels moving in and out of the Virginia Capes, bound for the ports of Hampton Roads, Baltimore, Bremen and Santos. It is the satisfied grunt of an Eastern Shoreman as he swings his tongs from an oyster bed.

The Bay is the Susquehanna Flats on a fall morning, the sand beaches on an August afternoon, the Norfolk Naval Shipyard at dusk, and the Calvert Cliffs flooded with moonlight.

The Bay is the scent of loblolly pine, the pencil-thin lines of the Bay bridge, the taste of real Maryland fried chicken and Smithfield ham, the quizzical expression of a waterman as he watches a Johns Hopkins University scientist test salinity of the water with a variety of test tubes and instruments.

The Bay is the Miles River Regatta, the Fishing Fair, the Hard Crab Derby, the Naval Academy's June Week and the jousting tournaments.

It is a mixture of Baltimore, Norfolk, Crisfield, Reedville, Yorktown, North Point, Gibson Island, Betterton, Old Point Comfort, Virginia, and Chance, Maryland.

Along the Chesapeake's shores are the United States Naval Academy, the Aberdeen Proving Ground, the world's largest tidewater steel mill, and, at Norfolk, the world's greatest naval base, plus the headquarters of the United States Atlantic Fleet and NATO's Supreme Allied Command, Atlantic.

The Chesapeake Bay is all this—and much more.

In measurable terms, it is probably the most impressive body of water in the United States. The Bay, which is 22 miles broad at its widest point, is 195 miles long. It has 48 main tributaries which are fed by 102 branches. The 150 rivers, creeks and branches are navigable for a distance of 1,750 miles. The total tidal shoreline of the Bay is an estimated 5,100 miles. The surface area of these waters is nearly four times the area of Rhode Island. The Bay's drainage system is nearly 65,000 square miles—almost equal to all of New England.

The Chesapeake is a great artery for ships from all over the world, it is the finest fishing hole in America, and one of the most fabulous playgrounds on the East Coast.

All manner of men live on its shores and along its rivers —the Eastern Shoreman (who can define him?), the millionaires who have bought up and restored many of the Colonial mansions, the tidewater families that trace their family trees back to the beginning of settlement in Virginia and Maryland, the We-Sorts who claim descent from the Indians, the Johnny-come-lately, and the visitor from the Mid-West who sees it only during a two weeks vacation but who loves it too.

Today the Bay and its country are in a process of change, and as a result the old is sometimes mixed incongruously with the new. The roar of jet planes taking off from the Patuxent Naval Air Test Center reverberates through seventeenth century houses held togther with wooden pegs. Tractors and yoke of oxen, until recently, worked in neighboring fields and forests. In the back country, ranch wagons bounce along oyster shell roads or cross a river on a hand-operated ferry. Rams which once hauled lumber sail no more.

The Bay is changing and yet the Bay has never really changed. After centuries it is still, as an early settler described it, "The Noblest Bay in the Universe."

BAY BRIDGE . . . Maryland's eastern and western shores are linked by the largest continuous entirely-over-water steel structure in the world. The bridge from shore to shore—from Sandy Point to Kent Island—measures 4.35 miles. The entire project, including approach roads, is 7.727 miles long. About 6,500,000 man hours of work and 60,000 tons of steel were needed to build it. Work began on November 3, 1949. The bridge was opened on July 30, 1952. It cost about $45,000,000 and will be paid for by tolls from this and other state bridges. The bridge was built in a graceful, sweeping curve to comply with regulations determined by the Corps of Engineers, U. S. Army, and to land the structure on favorable terrain. The photograph on the opposite page was made at dusk; the white streak was caused by automobile headlights. *Above,* oyster tongers at work on the south side of the bridge.

NATIONAL SHRINE . . .Fort McHenry, at the mouth of Baltimore's inner harbor, has been a national shrine since 1928. When the British fleet launched its attack on September 13, 1814, the out-sized flag that flew over the fort inspired Francis Scott Key, who watched the spectacular battle from a cartel ship in the harbor, to write the words of "The Star-Spangled Banner." The statue is in memory of Lieut. Col. George Armistead who commanded the fort during the two-day attack. The cannon are of 1860 vintage. The fort, which sits on Whetstone Point, attracts about 750,000 visitors annually.

THE HEART OF BALTIMORE . . . One of the glories of Baltimore—"Queen City of the Chesapeake"—is Mount Vernon Place which nestles quietly in the heart of the metropolis. The Doric column was the first monument started in honor of George Washington, but was not the first one completed. That honor goes to the stone tower near Boonsboro, Maryland. The cornerstone of the Baltimore monument was laid on July 4, 1815, but the monument was not completed until 1829. The statue of Washington faces the bustling harbor where ships from all over the world have docked since the middle of the eighteenth century.

FRIENDSHIP . . . A vast airport that ranks as one of the more modern in the world, Friendship International can accommodate everything from small sport planes to the largest jets in service. There are three major runways at Friendship, with the longest 9,450 feet, and the airport averages about 600 landings and take-offs a day.

Passenger traffic at Friendship, which increased more than 50 per cent in one recent two-year period, approaches 2,000,000 annually, and in 1965 the airport handled more than 38,000,000 pounds of freight. Located almost midway between Baltimore and Washington, Friendship has more than 100 jet flights daily.

THE CAPITOL . . . The site of the Capitol was selected by Major Pierre L'Enfant, who planned the city, because it seemed to him "a pedestal waiting for a monument." Once known as Jenkins' Heights, it is now called "The Hill." The plan for the Capitol was submitted by an amateur architect. The cornerstone was laid by Washington in 1793. The dome was added in the 1860's.

WASHINGTON, D.C. . . . The capital of the United States, on the Potomac River at the head of tide and navigation, was the first capital in the world planned exclusively as a seat of government. In this photograph, the railing of a bridge near the Jefferson Memorial seems to repeat over and over the pattern of the 555-foot Washington Monument, which was dedicated in 1885.

THE ANCIENT CITY . . . Annapolis, on the south bank of the Severn River, was the only capital deliberately laid out in colonial times primarily as a seat of government. For many years it was one of the political, cultural and social centers of America. Today its life centers around two bustling institutions—the State Government and the Naval Academy—but the beautiful city still retains much of its pre-Revolutionary flavor and charm. This is a view of Cornhill Street looking toward State Circle and the Capitol.

HOME PORT . . . From Eastport, across Spa Creek, the massive buildings of the United States Naval Academy form part of the Annapolis skyline. The Academy, first known as the Naval School, was opened at Fort Severn on October 10, 1845. The grounds of the Academy proper comprise some 294 acres along the west bank of the Severn River and contain 219 buildings.

THE CHASE-LLOYD HOUSE . . . Annapolis has many beautiful colonial mansions. One of the loveliest is the Chase-Lloyd House which was begun by Samuel Chase, a signer of the Declaration of Independence, in 1769, and completed by Edward Lloyd about 1774. Signers William Paca and Charles Carroll of Carrollton also are identified with Annapolis houses that remain.

41

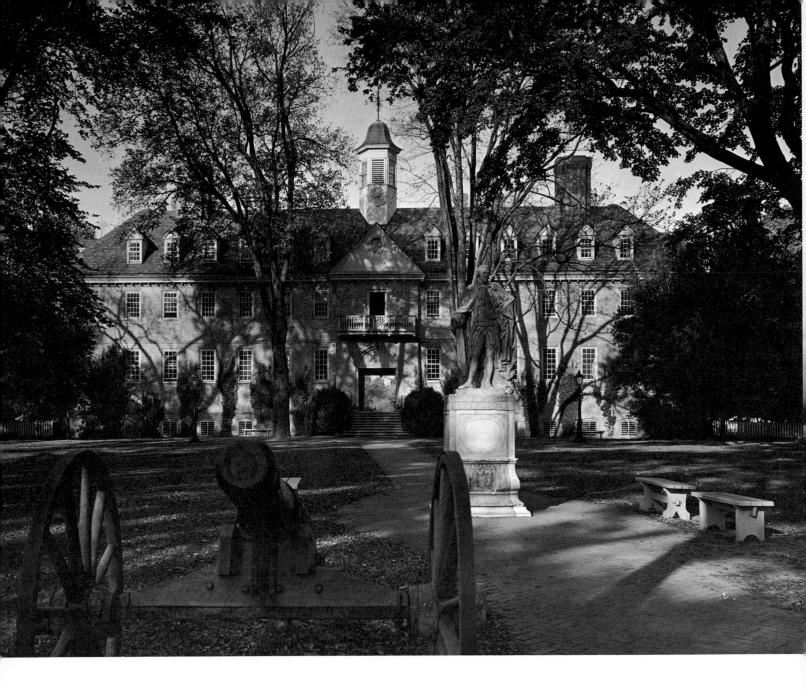

WILLIAM AND MARY . . . The College of William and Mary, founded in Williamsburg in 1693 by royal charter, is the second oldest college in America. It was the first to establish an elective system of study, an honor system, schools of law and modern languages, and the second to establish a school of medicine. The Phi Beta Kappa Society was founded here in 1776. The institution had a seat in the house of burgesses and was the only American college ever granted a coat of arms by the College of Heralds. Three presidents of the United States—Thomas Jefferson, James Monroe and John Tyler—were educated here. Pictured is the Wren Building, the only structure in America designed by Sir Christopher Wren, and the oldest academic building in the United States.   The building, begun in 1695, was burned three times, but the original walls were still standing when restoration was begun in 1928.

ST. JOHN'S COLLEGE . . . This venerable Annapolis institution, chartered in 1784, traces its lineage back to 1696 when its predecessor, King William's School, was founded. Early alumni included two of Washington's nephews, as well as Reverdy Johnson and Francis Scott Key. It once was so anti-coeducational that a president who favored coeducation was forced to resign. Now it seeks to attract women students. Since 1937 its curriculum has been based on the famous "Great Books" program. McDowell Hall is named for the first president of the college.

WASHINGTON COLLEGE . . . The Eastern Shore's oldest college—and eleventh oldest institution of learning in America—was founded by William Smith, an Anglican clergyman, in 1782 and named in honor of the then commander-in-chief of the Continental forces. Washington visited the college, which is on the banks of the Chester River in Chestertown, in 1784, and contributed 50 guineas to its endowment. Reid Hall is named in honor of Dr. Charles W. Reid, a former president, who made the school coeducational.

SENTINELS . . . Scattered throughout the Chesapeake and its tributaries are a great variety of lighthouses that have warned and guided mariners in all sorts of weather. From a distance some look like gigantic pop bottles bobbing rhythmically in the blue-green water, others like Victorian doll-houses on stilts or fat, prehistoric spiders. Many were given intriguing names: Wolf Trap, Old Plantation Flats, Windmill Point, Thimble Shoal. Once all were manned. Now, in a push-button age, automatic equipment has largely taken over.

DRUM POINT LIGHT

HOOPERS ISLAND LIGHT

HOLLAND ISLAND BAR LIGHT

THOMAS POINT LIGHT

SANDY POINT LIGHT

OXFORD . . . Lying on the southern tip of a peninsula between the Choptank and Tred Avon rivers, Oxford has one of the finest harbors on the Eastern Shore. The Maryland town had its beginnings in 1668, and the following year was designated as a port of entry. Because of its deep, land-locked harbor and its fine shipyards, Oxford soon became the chief port of entry and metropolis of the Shore. At one time nearly 200 vessels were registered at the Customs House. Large English commercial houses established branches here, exporting tobacco and importing slaves, indentured servants and convicts. When the tobacco trade fell off and other ports, such as Baltimore, grew, the decline of Oxford began. The last sea-going vessel called here in 1759. In 1793 a chronicler declared, "The once well-worn streets are now grown up in grass, save a few narrow tracks, made by sheep and swine, and the strands have more the appearance of an uninhabited island than where human feet had ever trod. . . . Bereft of all former greatness, nothing remains to console her but her salubrious air and fine navigation which may anticipate better times." Better times did come. Today Oxford is a commercial fishing and oystering center and also caters to sports fishermen and sailors. The view is of Morris Street—the main street—which was named in honor of Robert Morris, a tradesman, and his son who became the financier of the American Revolution, and later was sentenced to debtors' prison.

PARSON OF THE ISLANDS . . . Joshua Thomas was a dynamic young waterman who became a leader in Methodist revivals and camp meetings on the islands of Tangier Sound. Journeying from meeting to meeting in a log canoe named *The Methodist* he soon became famous as the "Parson of the Islands." Historians credit him with establishing Methodism as the deep-rooted faith of the island people. The most spectacular event of his career was preaching to the British expeditionary forces encamped on Tangier Island during the War of 1812—and predicting that they would not succeed in taking Baltimore. Thomas, who died in 1853, is buried here, in St. Johns Methodist graveyard, on Deals Island, right. The log canoe he used was a prototype of the *Island Blossom,* built in 1892, a famous racing log canoe, shown above with seven of the crew riding springboards to balance it.

SMITH ISLAND . . . This compact little archipelago of tidal marshes and "high ground" which lies just a few feet above high tide is Maryland's most remote and distinctive island. The 700 natives —most of whom are related—are divided into three communities: Tylerton, Rhodes Point and Ewell, the largest, shown at left. They live in trim white houses strung along narrow lanes which are used mainly for wheelbarrows and motor scooters. Most of the islanders are watermen and Democrats. All are Methodists and hardy, independent folk who love their isolated way of life (electricity didn't come until 1949) because it keeps them "close to nature and close to God."

SEAFOOD CAPITAL . . . Crisfield, which calls itself "Seafood Capital of the World," has a main street that is in reality one long wharf. The unique street, lined with weathered frame buildings, many with false top fronts, has a look of the Old West. Much of the lower town is built on millions of tons of oyster shells. Crisfieldians like to say that they "shipped out the oysters and lived on the shells." The unusual drawbridge connecting Main Street with the nearby island of Jersey is open more than it's closed, *right*. The mail boats that run to Smith and Tangier islands get ready to leave from the foot of Main Street, bottom picture.

DIVIDING LINE . . . At Smith Point, which lies along the Virginia-Maryland line just south of the Potomac River, the Chesapeake is some 22 miles broad—its widest point. It is one of the few Bay promontories that has a river discharging at its extremity—the Little Wicomico, about four miles in length, empties into the Bay between two stone jetties, one of which can be seen in the picture. Gilbert Klingel, naturalist and author of "The Bay," calls Smith Point, which has the largest osprey colony in the Maryland-Virginia tidewater country, "one of the most interesting areas in the entire Chesapeake."

IN HONOR OF . . . Two small towns on the Eastern Shore that owe their existence to the oyster are named in its honor. Bivalve, Maryland, top picture, is on the east bank of the Nanticoke River. The town once bore the prosaic name of Waltersville. Oyster, Virginia, above, is almost on the tip of the peninsula. The Shore has also villages called Oystershell and Shelltown.

DOUBLE CHIMNEYS . . . This early eighteenth century house stands on West St. Mary's Manor in Southern Maryland, once a 1,730 acre tract owned by Capt. Henry Fleet, fur trader and explorer who guided Leonard Calvert up the St. Marys River in 1634. The tiny window between the chimneys lights a small room. In manor days, four chimneys were a sign of affluence.

COURT LANE . . . A row of buildings on one side of the courthouse in Cambridge is known as "Court Lane." Some of the attorneys who occupy offices here jokingly call the street "Robber's Row." The courthouse which shadows the row is the third one on the site. The first was built in 1687 for 26,000 pounds of tobacco.

KENNERSLEY . . . "Finley Farm stands haggard on the pleasant meadows of Queen Annes County. A great tree fell in 1932 close to the front of the house, making it impossible to obtain a good photograph." So wrote Henry Chandlee Forman in his book "Early Manor and Plantation Houses of Maryland." In his photograph the house looked abandoned. Today the house, more commonly known as Kennersley, looks like this. It is on the Chester River near Church Hill, Maryland.

FROM A TINY ACORN . . . The Wye Oak in Talbot County is the official tree of Maryland and the State's most magnificent tree. It is 95 feet tall, has a spread of over 165 feet and measures 57 feet and seven inches around its trunk one foot from the ground. The State bought the tree and a small plot of ground around it in 1939 for $6,150 and constituted it a one-tree state forest, the only one in the nation.

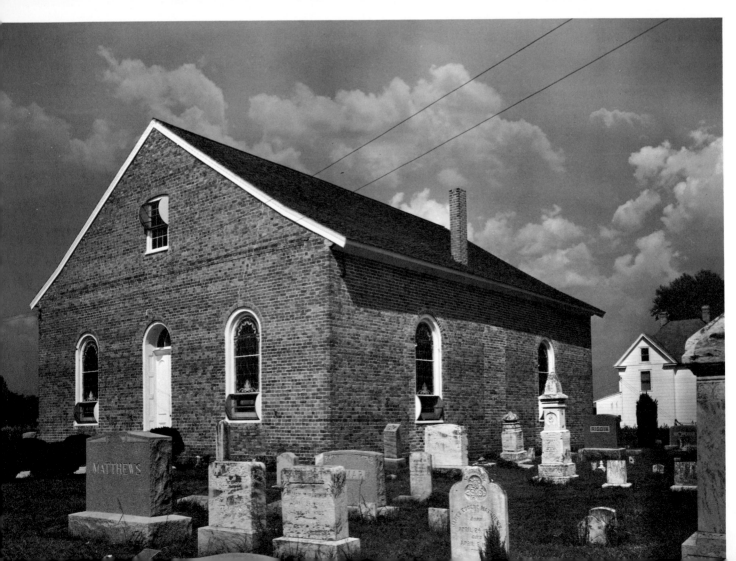

54

EARLY CHURCHES . . . Old Trinity Protestant Episcopal Church at Church Creek, Maryland, top left, was built before 1680. It will be restored through the generosity of Col. and Mrs. Edgar W. Garbisch. Rehobeth, bottom opposite page, was built about 1705, and is venerated as the oldest house of worship in the United States used exclusively by Presbyterians. It stands near Rehobeth, Maryland.

1682 AND 1695 . . . The Third Haven Meeting House in Easton, Maryland, *right,* was built in 1682-83, and is one of the oldest frame houses of worship in America. William Penn once held meetings under the oaks of an adjoining yard. *Below,* St. James Church in Anne Arundel County, Maryland, known locally as Herring Creek Church, belongs to an Anglican parish laid out in 1695. The restoration work has been termed "magnificent." In the churchyard are several tombstones dated 1666.

OLD WYE CHURCH . . . This lovely little church near the Wye Oak in Talbot County, Maryland, was completed in 1721. It was rededicated in July, 1949, after extensive renovation that was made possible through the generosity of a parishioner, Alfred Houghton, Jr., of Wye Plantation. The work took two years. The first Protestant Episcopal Church service in Maryland was believed to have been held on or near this site when Capt. William Claiborne and 25 settlers camped in this vicinity on August 17, 1631.

CARROLL MANSION . . . Charles Carroll of Carrollton, a Signer of the Declaration of Independence, was born and raised in the massive gabled house on the right. It was built by his father, Dr. Charles Carroll, in 1735. A large chapel on the third floor was the first Roman Catholic place of worship in Annapolis. The Victorian Gothic structure is St. Mary's Catholic Church on Duke of Gloucester Street; it was dedicated in 1860. The Carroll Mansion is now the House of the Second Novitiate of the Congregation of the Most Holy Redeemer, a Catholic religious order whose members are known as Redemptorists.

HAPPY HUNTING GROUNDS . . . The Calvert
Cliffs stretch for almost 30 miles along the western
shore of the Chesapeake, sometimes reaching a
height of more than 100 feet. They are classed as
one of the seven natural wonders of Maryland, and
are known throughout the world to paleontolo-
gists. From these cliffs came the first authenticated
deposits and fossils of the Miocene period in
America, the great middle period of the age of
mammals, millions of years ago. Every heavy rain
storm uncovers such things as crocodile teeth, rib
bones of whales and carapaces of sea turtles.

OSPREYS . . . A naturalist approaches two young ospreys, or fish hawks, in their nest on an island in the Chesapeake. The birds are found from Labrador to the Gulf of Mexico, and in Maryland and Virginia they breed in tidewater areas. One nestling banded in Maryland turned up eleven weeks later in Brazil.

PREY OF THE ELEMENTS . . . While the buildings that once were a keeper's quarters fall into ruin, an automatic light marks Cedar Point, just off the Patuxent Naval Air Test Station. Near here in the Patuxent River the submarine "escape lung" was developed by Charles B. Momsen, a naval officer, in 1928.

FIRING LINE . . . Hunters standing watch in a blind in the lower Bay get ready to fire as a flock of ducks appears in the distance. Canvasbacks, mallards, black ducks, pintails and scaup are among the species that make the Chesapeake one of the East's most famous waterfowl centers.

FOLLOWING THE HOUNDS . . . The first foxhunting in America was done as early as 1650 in Queen Annes County, Maryland. The sport was introduced by Robert Brooke who came from England in his own private ship with 28 servants and a pack of hounds. In 1730 eight pairs of English red foxes were liberated on the Eastern Shore. This marked the beginning in America of foxhunting in its present form. Many famous hunt clubs are to be found in the tidewater country of Maryland and Virginia.

BIRD NEST . . . Near famous Mulberry Grove on Taylors Island stands the LeCompte-Cator house which was built in the early part of the eighteenth century. In 1781 a newly organized Methodist congregation met here until a chapel was erected on the Maryland island. During the 1930's the house was used for storage. Now only its chimney is used—by birds.

GAME TIME . . . Whenever the weather was nice, men of leisure gathered on the porch of Maggie Wick's general store in Crisfield for a game of checkers. The black and red counters, once lost, were replaced by bottle caps. Years after this photograph was taken, the store was destroyed by fire.

MOUNT REPUBLICAN . . . This fine example of colonial architecture was built in 1792. It has walls 18 inches thick, and they are apparently as sturdy today as they were when Philadelphia was the capital of the United States. The brick mansion, which has a deep salmon color, stands at the head of an avenue of lovely trees overlooking the Potomac River. A one-time owner was Franklin Weems, one of the great *bon vivants* of Southern Maryland. Charles County legend has it that he always had his cellar filled with 50 barrels of brandy, and that he kept a poker game going in the house for 40 years. A great hunter, Weems maintained a pack of 100 fox hounds. Many of the best hunting dogs in the Potomac River country have the blood of these hounds in their veins.

HABRE-de-VENTURE . . . This house, built on the arc of an imaginary circle, is unique among tidewater mansions. The three principal types of Southern Maryland houses are exemplified in the five-part structure—an all brick house, an all frame house, and a frame house with brick gable-ends. The house, near Port Tobacco, was built about ten years before the Revolution, and was the home of Thomas Stone, a Signer of the Declaration of Independence. His grave is near the house. An early copy of the Declaration of Independence, identical in size and appearance with the original, was presented by Congress to the Stone family and it hung for many years in the drawing room. The beautiful hand carved paneling in that room and the corner cupboards were removed in 1928 and set up in a colonial room of the Baltimore Museum of Art as the finest exhibit of paneling that could be found in Maryland.

X MARKS THE SPOT . . . The Smith house, right, is on the site of Johnson's Tavern which, because of its strategic location straddling the Maryland-Delaware line, was the headquarters of "Patty" Cannon, a notorious murderer, robber and kidnapper of free Negroes. She committed suicide in 1829 after confessing that she killed eleven persons, and helped kill at least twelve others.

CROSS MANOR . . . On the bank of St. Inigoes' Creek, not far from St. Marys City, stands the oldest brick house in Maryland. It was built by Capt. Thomas Cornwallis, one of the richest men in the colony, about 1643.

TEACKLE MANSION . . . This mansion in Princess Anne was begun in 1801 by Littleton Teackle, a banker and shipping magnate. The house is almost 200 feet long, and it is insulated with sawdust and shavings. The rear of the house, which initially was the front, faces the Manokin River. The house figures in George Townsend's book, "The Entailed Hat."

MAKEPEACE . . . This house on Johnson Creek near Crisfield was built in 1664 by John Roach and is said to have been surrounded at one time by a high brick wall as protection against Indians. It has 16-inch thick brick walls worked in a diamond pattern, and its two fireplaces are among the noblest in Maryland, each measuring 10 feet wide.

MULBERRY GROVE . . . Overlooking an estuary of the Potomac River at Port Tobacco, this was the home of Marylander John Hanson, first President of the United States in Congress Assembled. It was built in the early 1700's and was reconstructed in 1934 after being swept by fire. The great double chimneys at one end are characteristic of a Colonial mansion.

ROSE HILL . . . Considered one of the finest homes in Maryland because of its regularity of design and architectural excellence, Rose Hill near Port Tobacco once was the home of Dr. Gustavus Brown, one of the physicians who attended George Washington during his last illness. Built in 1730, the house still has the original floors and woodwork.

LAWRENCE . . . Near Seaford is a mansion with a portico of tall square columns and wings with interesting shapes. Known as Lawrence, the well-preserved Delaware mansion was built about 1840 by Charles Wright, one of three Maryland brothers who prospered as traders and shippers during Seaford's lusty growth.

NYLON CAPITAL OF THE WORLD . . . Seaford, Delaware, is called that because here, in 1937, du Pont built the first plant in the world to manufacture nylon. The trim little city is at the head of navigation on the tuckahoe-lined Nanticoke River, about 40 miles from its mouth in the lower Chesapeake. Seaford was laid out in 1799.

HOME OF THE RAM . . . Bethel, Delaware, sits quietly along Broad Creek, a tributary of the Nanticoke River. In the words of the guide book, it is "a forgotten backwater of the Bay." Once it was a busy and famous shipbuilding town which developed the ram, a sturdy but narrow, wall-sided centerboard craft with three masts.

CANNON'S FERRY . . . The only cable ferry left in Delaware crosses the Nanticoke River at Woodland. The ferry, named for the man who built the large house in the background, is powered by an automobile engine fastened to one side. Until 1930 the ferryman pulled it across the river by hand.

RICHMOND . . . The capital of Virginia and the former capital of the Confederacy stands at the head of navigation on the James River. Although it is some 80 miles inland from Norfolk, it is a United States Customs Port of Entry that annually handles exports such as scrap iron and steel and imports such as petroleum and ore valued at more than $15,000,000. The State Capitol, above, houses one of the world's oldest representative legislatures.

JAMES FORT . . . One of the features of Festival Park on Jamestown Island is the fort, below, which was built to show what life was like in the early days of the settlement. Costumed guides show visitors the mud-and-thatch houses and ramparts of the fort. At the time of the landing at Jamestown in 1607 this was a peninsula, not an island, but erosion has taken about 25 acres of the western section of the townsite. The island now is a flat oval of marsh and woodland three miles long.

COLONIAL CAPITOL . . . This pink brick structure is a reconstruction of the first capitol at Williamsburg and is built on the original foundations of "colonial America's most important building." Here Patrick Henry delivered his fiery attack on the Stamp Act, and Virginia issued her famous call for American independence. The H-shaped building was one of 189 reconstructed and 77 restored during the restoration of Colonial Williamsburg. The unique restoration plan was visualized by the late Dr. W. A. R. Goodwin, rector of Bruton Parish Church, and was accomplished with the financial assistance of John D. Rockefeller, Jr.

THE PALACE . . . This is an authentic reproduction of the palace erected as a residence for the royal governors shortly after Williamsburg became the capital of the English colony. Contemporaries called the stately mansion, which was the center of Virginia social life, "the best in all English America." The palace is seen here from the extensive gardens, which also were reconstructed. The woman in eighteenth century dress is one of the many attendants who is employed by Colonial Williamsburg, Inc.

FORT MONROE . . . Jefferson Davis, president of the Confederacy, was held a political prisoner in a casemate of these granite walls of Fort Monroe from 1865 to 1867. The casemate, with its whitewashed walls, pine floor and barred window overlooking the green waters of the moat, has been restored to its 1865 appearance. It attracts thousands of visitors to the fort on Old Point Comfort, Virginia.

VICTORY MONUMENT . . . Rising high above the Yorktown National Park is an ornate marble column commemorating the victory of American and French forces over the British army of Cornwallis, which brought the Revolutionary War to an end. Lightning once struck the figure of Liberty atop the column and for years the head and arms were missing.

MOUNT VERNON . . . "No estate in United America is more pleasantly situated than this. It lyes . . . on one of the finest Rivers in America. . . . " That description of Mount Vernon, which sits on a Virginia ridge overlooking the Potomac, was written by George Washington who lived here from 1754 to his death in 1799.

POHICK CHURCH . . . George Washington was one of the vestrymen who in 1769 picked the site of Pohick Church on a slope overlooking the Potomac River, a few miles below Mount Vernon. The church was completed in 1774. It has been twice renovated, and is regarded as one of the finer Colonial churches.

POE SHRINE . . . The gray stone cottage, built about 1686, is the oldest house in Richmond. It is now a shrine in memory of Edgar Allan Poe who spent his childhood and young manhood in the Virginia capital. On exhibition are some Poe manuscripts and other objects associated with his early life. Behind the house is a sheltered garden.

WESTOVER . . . Once the home of the Byrd family, Westover is one of the earliest Virginia houses built on the grand scale. The dark red brick mansion, which overlooks the James River, bears a resemblance to the Governor's Palace in Williamsburg. The overthrow between the two posts holding leaden eagles is regarded as the finest piece of old English ironwork in America.

ACCOMAC . . . This solid little building was once the debtors' prison in Accomac, seat of Accomack County on the Eastern Shore of Virginia. It was built about 1731. Accomac was first known as Drummond in honor of Richard Drummond on whose land the town was laid out in 1786. Accomack is an Indian word meaning "other-side place" or "other side of water place."

LEE'S BIRTHPLACE . . . In this mansion which stands on cliffs high above the Potomac River in Virginia's Westmoreland County, Robert E. Lee was born on January 19, 1807, the son of Henry Lee, governor of Virginia and a Revolutionary War hero. The mansion, known as Stratford, was begun in 1729. It is architecturally famous for the two arcaded groups of four chimneys. The Robert E. Lee Memorial Foundation, which now owns Stratford, has restored the estate to provide a model colonial plantation and to serve as a memorial to Lee, commander of the Confederate forces and one of the great military commanders of our country. Lee's political creed may be summed up in the words he wrote just before war erupted—"I can anticipate no greater calamity for the country than the dissolution of the Union. . . . Still a union that can only be maintained by swords and bayonets, and in which strife and civil war are to take the place of brotherly love and kindness, has no charms for me. If the Union is dissolved and the government dispersed I shall return to my native state and share the miseries of my people and, save in defence, will draw my sword no more." Lee lost no stature following his surrender at Appomattox. He was one of the few famous military commanders who had the respect of both the vanquished and the victors.

BERKELEY . . . This beautiful early Georgian mansion on the James River is said to be the oldest three-story brick house in Virginia. It was built in 1726 by Benjamin Harrison whose son of the same name was a member of the Continental Congress, a Signer of the Declaration of Independence and thrice governor of Virginia. It is also the ancestral home of two United States presidents, William Henry Harrison and Benjamin Harrison. As such it has a distinction shared only with the Adams House in Massachusetts. During the War Between States, General McClellan used Berkeley as his headquarters while the Army of the Potomac was encamped nearby. "Taps" was composed here at that time.

MOUNT AIRY . . . River mansions built of stone are unusual because the tidewater country lacked that material. Mount Airy, near Tappahannock, Virginia, on the Rappahannock River, is an outstanding example of the stone house. It was built in 1758 by Col. John Tayloe whose son maintained a band of musicians among his servants. Francis Lightfoot Lee, who married a daughter of the builder, is buried on the grounds.

CARTER'S GROVE . . . The mansion, opposite page, is on the James River. It was built between June and September of 1751 at a cost of 500 pounds. It once belonged to "King" Carter who owned 300,000 acres and 1,000 slaves. Among his descendants were eight Virginia governors, three signers of the Declaration of Independence, and two United States presidents. Now entrusted to Colonial Williamsburg, this estate is open to the public daily, March through November.

KERR PLACE . . . This formal two-story Georgian brick mansion was built in 1779 by John Sheppard Kerr of Scotland on a 1,500-acre tract in Onancock on the Eastern Shore of Virginia. The walls of the drawing room were papered originally with life-size pictures of one of the Caesars. The building, excellently preserved, is the home of the Eastern Shore of Virginia Historical Society. The drawing room chandelier is a duplicate of one in the Governor's Palace in Williamsburg.

MOORE HOUSE . . . In this house near Yorktown, Virginia, commissioners representing American, French and British forces met on October 18, 1781, to arrange the articles of capitulation for Lord Cornwallis' British army. The house, beautifully restored, was built before 1750.

EYRE HALL . . . This rambling frame house near East-ville, Virginia, was the center of the Eyre estate which once extended across the lower Eastern Shore. The main section was built in the last quarter of the eighteenth century. Behind the house is a buttery and one of the oldest and loveliest box gardens in Northampton County.

DEPENDENCIES . . . In ancient times, behind every mansion stood a row of small houses known as dependencies. They served as summer kitchens, spin-ninghouse, washhouse, coach-house, storehouse, and, on the larger estates, as schoolhouse, shops for the shoemaker and tail-or and offices for the gardener and butler. These trim little dependencies are at Kendall Grove, an estate near Birdsnest, on the Eastern Shore of Virginia.

OAK GROVE . . . The Oak Grove Methodist Church, near Keller on the Eastern Shore of Virginia, has a Sunday School dating from 1785, which is said to be the oldest continuous church school in the United States. Oak Grove started under the name of Burton's Chapel. It is one of the earliest Methodist congregations on the Eastern shore.

HUNGARS CHURCH . . . This church, at Bridgetown, on the Eastern Shore of Virginia, was once the longest and second largest of all the churches in the commonwealth. It was built in 1742 and it is the third church of that name. The walls are two feet thick. It has undergone a number of architectural changes; the major one was shortening the structure by 20 feet. The church is said to have had the first pipe organ in America.

BRIDGE OF BOATS . . . When the tonging fleet that sails out of Deep Creek and Menchville, Virginia, is anchored in Deep Creek it literally forms a bridge of boats between the two towns. At times there are 1,000 boats riding at anchor. The fleet tongs for seed oysters in the James River.

MOTHBALL FLEET . . . More than a hundred ships, most of them World War II Liberties, are anchored in the James River as part of the U. S. Merchant Marine reserve fleet. In June, 1953, fifty Liberties were used to store some 8,000,000 bushels of surplus grain.

WASHINGTON WORKED HERE . . . Dr. Hugh Mercer settled in Fredericksburg, Virginia, on the advice of George Washington, a close friend, and practiced medicine and conducted his apothecary shop in this building. Washington kept a desk here for transacting business when he journeyed up to Fredericksburg, which is at the head of navigation on the Rappahannock River.

HOME OF THE SMITHFIELD HAM . . . Smithfield, Virginia, on the Pagan River, is an important peanut market and the world-famous producer of the delicious Smithfield hams. The best hams come from hogs that roam in fields and woods until fall when they are turned loose in peanut fields to fatten. The peanuts and an ancient curing method give the dark-red hams their distinctive flavor.

CHINCOTEAGUE'S WILD PONIES . . . Clam diggers, oystermen and fishermen turn cowboys once each year to roundup the ponies that run wild on Assateague Island which is on the Atlantic side of Virginia's Eastern Shore. The men, in boats and on horseback, make the ponies swim the 400-foot channel from Assateague to Chincoteague Island. There, in a famous summer event known as Pony Penning, the small, shaggy ponies are auctioned off. Sometimes as many as a 100 are sold, and some bring $125. According to tradition, the ponies are descendants of Spanish horses that were shipwrecked off the coast hundreds of years ago. Another explanation is that they are offspring of ponies that strayed from Virginia plantations.

TANGIER ISLAND . . . Most of it is marsh, yet about 1,000 people—perhaps a third of them named Crockett—live on the high ground less than five feet above high tide. Twelve homemade bridges span the sluices that lace the beautiful island. Tangier, just below the Virginia line, ranks with neighboring Smith as the most picturesque of the Bay's islands. Only recently did Tangier begin to succumb to the influences of the modern world. Boats now carry sightseers to the island and Tangier has telephones, television and motor scooters, which have supplanted bicycles as the main means of transportation on the oyster shell roads. Tombstones still can be seen in front yards, but most burials now are in a cemetery.

CHESAPEAKE BAY WATERMAN

Bay Life

CAPTAIN'S PARADISE . . . Gwynn's Island, Virginia, is a seafood center which is said to have produced more sea captains in World War II than any other Bay community. Here in 1776 Lord Dunmore, the royal governor, made his last stand against the Virginia patriots whose cannon on Cricket Hill drove his fleet away.

RAIL BIRDING . . . Hunters searching for rail birds in the Patuxent marshes use long narrow skiffs which were especially designed to get through the wild oats and heavy marsh grasses. The skiffs are poled by pushers who get $10 "for working a tide," about four hours work. They can be used only with the tides for there is just enough water then to get them through. The rail bird season in Maryland extends from September 1 through October 20. The daily limit of the Carolina rail, also called sora, is 25. About three or four make a meal for one.

WHITE BEAUTY . . . Every year thousands of majestic whistling swan fly out of the Great Lakes region to winter in the Chesapeake Bay country. Their favorite feeding grounds are the Susquehanna Flats and the shallow waters of the upper tributaries. This photograph was made from a United States Fish and Wildlife Service airplane which was engaged in making a survey of ducks, geese and swan. Wildlife authorities estimate that some 15,000 swan winter in the Chesapeake.

FISHERMEN'S PARADISE . . . As this picture indicates, sports fishing in the Bay is enjoyed by men, children and women. It is estimated that some 300,000 people fish for fun every year in the Bay. No license is required. Some fish from pilings, others from rowboats, runabouts or cabin cruisers. Striped bass (rock) white and yellow perch, and shad are the most popular catches. The fishermen's big event is the Fishing Fair held on the eastern and western shores on alternate years.

CONSERVATION . . . Haul seiners working in the Bay are checked by an inspector who taxied his plane up to the net. Maryland Marine Police inspectors now use a helicopter instead of a plane. They also use 42 cabin cruisers, ranging from 27 to 63 feet in length, and 45 outboards in what is known as the "oyster navy."

SHAD RUN . . . Scores of fishermen swarm along the Potomac near Washington's Chain Bridge for the spring shad run. In this gorge the fish congregate by the million. The stretch of river is so jammed with fish that some anglers simply throw in bare hooks to snag their catch. Others use dip nets or their bare hands.

LAZY DAYS . . . There are many joys to be experienced while sailing on the Chesapeake. Certainly one of the finest is just relaxing on a gently rising and falling deck, watching the grandeur of sky and water and a sunset playing on the face of a pretty girl—and at the same time wiggling the toes in utter freedom and contentment.

SHOOTING STARS . . . The trim, fast star boat is one of the most popular sailboats on the Chesapeake. It is 22 feet, 8 inches in length. Two international star boat regattas have been held on the Bay. The first star appeared in the Chesapeake after World War I.

POWER AND BEAUTY . . . Power boats now outnumber sailboats on the Bay. They range in cost from a few hundred dollars to around $100,000 for the 60-foot luxury models. A power boat is defined as a craft at least sixteen feet long with an inboard motor.

DRESS PARADE . . . This photograph of the entire brigade of the United States Naval Academy—some 3,400 midshipmen—was taken from a helicopter and is the first such picture ever made. In autumn and spring, the entire brigade drills at dress parades on Worden Field on Wednesdays from 3:25 to 3:55 P.M., weather permitting. In the background is the dome of the State Capitol, the oldest state capitol still in use.

TEST CENTERS . . . Sabre and Banshee jets, *left,* rest on the aprons at the mammoth Patuxent Air Test Center at Cedar Point, Maryland. Some days the center, which was opened in 1943, has as many as 2,000 landings and takeoffs. Below, gun barrels await tests at the Aberdeen Proving Ground, called "the world's largest shooting gallery." Situated on the west side of the upper Bay, Aberdeen covers 74,435 acres in an area about six miles wide and eighteen miles long. The proving ground is the hub of army ordnance activities for the research, development and testing of arms, ammunition, tanks, combat vehicles and motor transportation for the Armed Forces.

A Hunter's Best Friends . . . A good dog and a decoy maker play a big role in waterfowl shooting. A Chesapeake Bay retriever waits patiently between two hunters, left. The Ward brothers, Steve and Lem, above, are world famed as waterfowl carvers. In a busy year about a quarter century ago, the brothers turned out 800 shooting stools which sold for $1.25 each. Today a pair of what Lem calls his "fancy ducks" will bring as much as $500, and he is a year and a half behind in filling orders. The men are masters of a disappearing art.

Distant Buck . . . This photograph of a deer at Aberdeen Proving Ground was made with a telephoto lens from a distance of nearly one-third of a mile. The figure of the animal on the negative was so small that to enlarge it for reproduction it was necessary to remodel the enlarging apparatus. Thousands of deer roam the proving ground safe from hunters.

WING TO WING . . . With the wind behind them, two graceful log canoes sail down the Bay, wing to wing. The log canoe is a development of the Indian dugout which was hollowed from a gigantic log with stone and fire. Settlers found it simpler to build their canoes from two or three logs rather than from a single great one. Eventually sails and centerboards were added. The famous canoe *Magic* is on the left.

TAKEOFF . . . A broken spinnaker swings free from the *Highland Light* during a race on the Chesapeake. The 68-foot ocean-racing sloop was built at Neponsett, Maine, in 1931, and was presented to the Naval Academy in 1939.

DRIVING TO WIN . . . The Bay's broad waters mean play as well as work to Annapolis midshipmen. With the 72-foot ketch *Vamarie* and other craft they enter many sailing races on the Chesapeake—and some on the Atlantic. The *Vamarie* holds the record for one New England-Bermuda event. This boat was presented to the Naval Academy by a one-time Czarist naval officer.

DUCK HUNTING . . . Tidewater Maryland provides some of the finest waterfowl hunting in the country, and experienced gunners usually have their decoys bobbing in the water around them as the first hues of early morning pink tint the sky.

RACERS . . . Three racing yachts streak down the Bay in the Chesapeake Skipper invitation 100-mile race which is from the Severn River to Point-No-Point Lighthouse and return. The trip has been made in seventeen hours. One year it took almost 30 hours. There are 60 major yachting centers on the Bay which race everything from the tiny moths to the Class A unlimited yachts.

POCOMOKE RIVER . . . The most unusual waterway on the Eastern Shore, the 70-mile Pocomoke is almost tropical in mood and appearance in places. It is noted for its black water, its depth (35 feet in spots) and its almost impenetrable swamp. Great cypress trees, such as the one at right, fringe its banks.

99

SAFE HARBOR . . . Scenes like the above are common on the Chesapeake Bay where sailing is one of the major recreational pursuits and the shores are dotted with yacht clubs, boat clubs and marinas. Craft ranging from penguins to ocean-going yachts can be seen on Bay waters practically year round.

WEEKEND RACES . . . Races sponsored by yacht clubs attract hundreds of competitors on Saturdays and Sundays when the Chesapeake echoes with starting guns and shouted commands. The crews in the boats above jockey for an advantageous position moments before crossing the starting line.

NAVY YAWLS . . . U.S. Naval Academy yawls crewed by midshipmen sweep across the Chesapeake on the final leg of a Sunday race, top, while the sailboat, right, heels sharply after rounding a marker during a regatta. A power craft, known as a committee boat, carries the officials responsible for judging such races, and it can move swiftly to enable those aboard to watch much of the drama unfold.

MEN OF THE BAY COUNTRY . . . Chesapeake Bay watermen, and those in related crafts, have earned a reputation for being God-fearing, hardworking, rugged individualists. The four pictured on these two pages are excellent examples of the Bay man. Top left, Melvin Collier, a Deals Island blacksmith, was famous for his oyster dredges—pronounced "drudges" on the Shore. Watermen said that dredges, which Collier made freehand, had a "magic touch." Bottom left, Capt. Will Jones, of Cambridge, was owner and captain of the *J. T. Leonard*, the last working sloop on the Bay. The captain, who dredged oysters for more than 50 years, was 81 when the picture was taken. Below, a weathered waterman from Mathews County, Virginia, mends his net after returning from many hours of fishing on the Bay.

SAILMAKER . . . Albert Brown works on a skipjack's sail in his loft, which is the largest full-scale one on the Eastern Shore. The loft, in Wenona, Maryland, was established in 1870, and the fourth generation of Browns now works there. The Browns make and repair sails for the Bay's commercial sailing craft and for yachtsmen along the coast from Maine to Florida.

DIAMOND-BACK TERRAPIN . . . Tidewater cooking ranks with the best in the country. One of the most famous dishes is diamond-back terrapin, Maryland style. This is the way to prepare it: Immerse live terrapin in boiling water and boil under cover until tender. Withdraw from water, placing terrapin on back to retain natural essence. When cool remove yellow shell skin. Use all meat portions, eggs and liver. Do not let any of gall bladder penetrate meat or essence. To each 6-inch terrapin use ¼ pound of butter and ½ cup of sherry.

from Fred Stieff's "Eat, Drink And Be Merry In Maryland"

CRAB NORFOLK . . . A good tidewater cook knows at least 20 ways to prepare crabs. A favorite dish in the lower Bay area is Crab Norfolk. This is the way it's made: One pound crab meat, ¼ pound butter, 1¼ tablespoons vinegar, salt, red and black pepper. Mix seasonings with crabmeat gently. Place in casserole, dot with butter, cover and bake in oven 350 degrees F. for 20 to 30 minutes.

from "A Cook's Tour of the Eastern Shore of Maryland"

MARYLAND BEATEN BISCUITS . . . One of the most unusual—and tastiest—items of Bay cookery is the Maryland beaten biscuit. This is a good recipe for it: ½ pint flour, 1/3 teaspoon lard, 1/3 teaspoon salt. Sift salt into flour. Rub lard in thoroughly and add ½ gill milk and ½ gill water to make a very stiff dough. Knead for five minutes then beat with a hatchet or heavy stick for a half hour or more. Shape into biscuits, prick tops and bake in moderate oven for 20 minutes.

from A. Aubrey Bodine's "My Maryland"

WHITE POTATO PIE . . . The lower area of the Eastern Shore produces large yields of potatoes. One of the favorite dishes there, of course, is white potato pie. The recipe for Snow Hill White Potato Pie: 3 cups mashed potatoes, 1½ cups fresh milk, 1 cup condensed milk, 3 eggs, ¾ cup sugar, 2 tablespoons melted butter, 2 teaspoons lemon extract, cinnamon and nutmeg. Cream butter and sugar thoroughly. Add beaten egg yolks, then potatoes. Stir in milk, lemon, cinnamon and nutmeg, and finally the beaten egg whites. Pour into uncooked 9-inch pie shell and bake in 350 degree F. oven for 1 hour.

from Snow Hill Inn, Snow Hill, Maryland

MARYLAND FRIED CHICKEN . . . This famous dish is known throughout the United States and is often seen on menus in foreign countries. One of the best ways to prepare it is: Cut up a young, tender chicken. "Dredge" with flour, then fry in a deep fat to a golden brown. Serve on a layer of fried cornmeal mush or johnny-cake with cream gravy.

from A. Aubrey Bodine's "My Maryland"

CRAB FEAST . . . A crab feast consists of a heaping supply of hard crabs, steamed a bright red, and plenty of cold beer. Eating is highly informal. Crabs are usually served on a table covered with newspapers, and the only utensils are paring knives and nutcrackers. Men roll up their sleeves and don aprons. It is not unusual for a tidewater native to eat a dozen crabs at one sitting. When crabs are steamed they are seasoned with vinegar, salt, dry mustard, tabasco, red and black pepper.

OYSTER ROAST . . . The first oyster roast of the fall usually follows hard on the last crab feast. At a good roast, oysters are served in a variety of ways—on the half shell, fried, steamed and in stew. Supplementing the oyster are such things as steamed shrimp, cold cuts, turkey, sauerkraut, hot dogs, pigs in the blanket, and, of course, draft beer. Tickets to some oyster roasts cost as much as $7.50. More politicking is done at an oyster roast than any other affair, with the possible exception of a national convention.

OLDEST SOCIAL CLUB . . . The South River Club claims
to be the oldest social organization with a continuous life in
the United States. Though no definite proof exists, members believe the club was founded about 1700. The purpose of the club is the enjoyment by "a group of men of
genial and congenial tastes, background and character" of
"good eating, drinking, conversation and fellowship." The
club has four dinners a year in a tiny 212-year-old club-
house on the banks of the South River near Annapolis.
Membership is limited to 25 men.

ANNAPOLIS YACHT CLUB . . . Once known as the Severn Boat Club, the Annapolis Yacht Club is one of the oldest in the country and traces its origin to 1886. It has about 1,200 members, almost 75 per cent of whom own boats, and overlooks Spa Creek and the colorful Annapolis harbor. The present building, which some members refer to as "Japanese Colonial" in style, was completed in 1963 at a cost of $500,000. The club is the starting point in alternate years for the classic yacht race between Annapolis and Newport.

AUDIENCE AFLOAT . . . Sunday sailors aboard a cruising class vessel watch with interest as midshipmen rig a Naval Academy yawl. Middies gain their sea legs racing and cruising on the Chesapeake and its many inviting tributaries, such as the Tred Avon, Choptank and Miles rivers.

LESSONS IN SEAMANSHIP . . . Cadets from the U.S. Coast Guard Academy throw their weight into a line aboard the training bark *Eagle* on a visit to the Chesapeake Bay. The 295-foot three-masted sailing ship, which is square-rigged, accommodates about 300 cadets on summer training cruises. The *Eagle's* home port is New London, Connecticut.

PLAYGROUND . . . The Chesapeake is a fabulous summer playground for the native and visitors who are attracted by the miles of magnificent beaches, wonderful fishing and some of the best sailing waters in the Western Hemisphere. Water skiing is one of the most popular water sports.

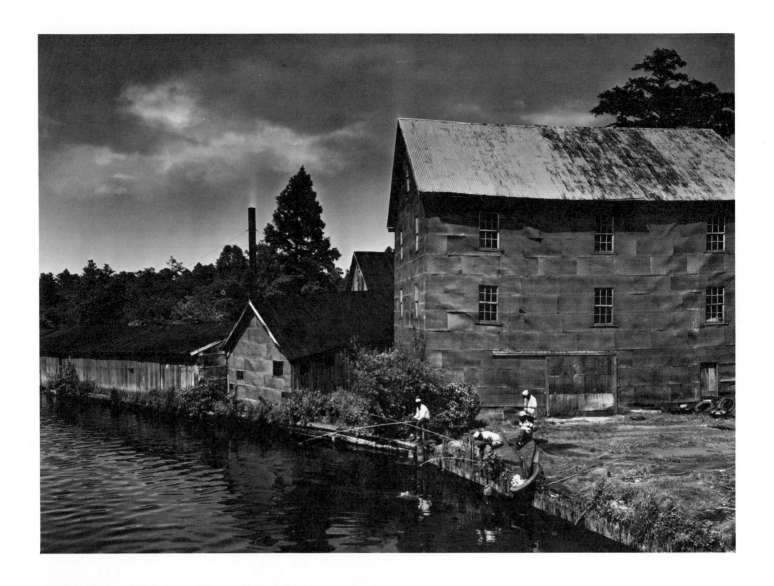

THE FULL LIFE . . . Life is leisurely and full in the tidewater river towns. This is a view of the Pocomoke River, just a few feet away from the downtown section of Pocomoke City, Maryland. Vessels from here once carried barrel and hogshead staves to the West Indies and brought back molasses, sugar, coffee and rum.

MULE POWER . . . The Shad Point Marine Railway on the Wicomico River near Salisbury, Maryland, now utilizes conventional power but once was a mule-propelled marine railway. The mule walked in a circle pulling a beam connected to cogwheels which drew boats out of the water. It took the mule about an hour to pull a boat up the 90-foot track.

TOBACCO . . . Two hundred years ago, tobacco was the big crop of the Bay country. Now, practically none is grown on the Eastern Shore or between the Potomac and James rivers in Virginia. The five southern counties of Maryland produce most of the tidewater tobacco today. This is a barn where tobacco is air cured.

SHORTCUT . . . The fourteen-mile Chesapeake and Delaware Canal, which connects the bays of those names, is a vital link in the inland waterway and it shortens the water route between Philadelphia and Baltimore by some 280 miles. The canal was predicted as early as 1661, but was not built until the 1820's. It once had locks but it is now a sea-level route handling deep-draft ships.

Capes to Canal

ARTERY . . . The Chesapeake Bay, 195 miles in length from the Virginia Capes to the mouth of the Susquehanna River, is one of the great arteries of world trade, serving the bustling ports of Baltimore and Hampton Roads. The Bay, which curves so slightly that a ship's course up the channel to Swan Point varies no more than two points of the compass, is a roadway for all manner of vessel, ranging from the skipjack with patched sails to the *N.S. Savannah,* the world's first nuclear-powered merchant ship. Just inside the capes is the boat of the Maryland Pilots Association which furnishes pilots for the run to Baltimore and from there to the Chesapeake and Delaware Canal. It is the longest pilotage in the country. On the right is the lighthouse at Cape Henry. It was the first one built by the United States government after we became a nation. Dating to 1791, it was acquired by the Association for the Preservation of Virginian Antiques.

BALTIMORE, WORLD PORT . . . Baltimore is one of the five major North Atlantic ports of the United States and it is often described as the most southern of the northern ports, the most northern of the southern ports and the most western of the eastern ports. The port actually predates the city. Baltimore became an important port and trading center during the Revolutionary War and achieved international recognition in the eighteenth century when its speedy Clippers were bringing coffee from South America, tea from China and slaves from Africa. In recent decades, it has developed into one of the world's great ports. To-day, the port and its closely allied facilities constitute the largest single industry in Baltimore. On the opposite page is the inner harbor and the Baltimore skyline which is dominated by the 34-story Maryland National Bank Build-ing. In all, the city has some 40 miles of waterfront.

HARBOR ACTIVITY . . . A tug guides a large freighter in one of the main shipping channels in the Baltimore harbor, while a dredge works at left. Goods moving in and out of the port are received from or directed to some 120 nations.

YESTERDAY AND TODAY . . . The past and the present—here the ram and the diesel-engined tanker—meet often on the Bay. Sometimes it is a radar-directed task force and a log canoe heading for Annapolis, or a weather-worn skipjack and a new freighter moored at the same pier.

LAZARETTO POINT . . . Bay buoys fill a pier at the Coast Guard Station on Lazaretto Point which is directly across from Fort McHenry. During the War of 1812, chains were stretched between the two points to keep British ships from entering Baltimore's inner harbor. In the background is the U.S.S. Roberts, a destroyer escort used by Naval Reservists.

DIVERSIFIED CARGO . . . Bulk cargo is the mainstay of the world port of Baltimore, but each year the role played by general cargo increases as new facilities are provided to handle a growing list of products. Baltimore also is fast becoming a specialist in handling project shipments such as dismantled steel mills to points overseas.

OIL AND WATER AT CANTON . . . Giant tankers lie at the piers of the Esso Standard Oil refinery and storage site, off Boston Street, discharging cargo. Crude petroleum and petroleum products, which represent one of the port's largest bulk commodities, come to Baltimore from many domestic and foreign points.

FROM ADEN TO YOKOHAMA . . . More than 100 overseas and coastal steamship lines have approximately 350 general cargo sailings monthly from Baltimore to such distant ports as Aden, Kobe, Antwerp, Bombay, Mobile, Mombasa, Bremen, Karachi, Liverpool, Portland, Cape Town and Yokohama.

HARBOR SCENE . . . Baltimore, in addition to being the nation's chief metallic ore import center, is also the leading East Coast port for grain, fertilizer and chemicals, and a major handler of coal and oil. This is a typical early morning view. The American Sugar Refining Co. Baltimore plant is in the background.

WORLD'S LARGEST . . . Just outside of Baltimore, on the Patapsco River close to its entry into the Bay, is the Sparrows Point plant of the Bethlehem Steel Company, the world's largest steel plant. The plant covers 2,000 acres and has an ingot capacity of about 9,000,000 tons. It imports in excess of 10,000,000 tons of ore annually from Canada, Africa, Venezuela and Chile.

MARINE TERMINALS . . . In one respect, Baltimore differs from all other U.S. seaports. Practically all of the large marine terminals are owned or operated by the trunk lines and terminal railroads serving the port. *Right,* cargo is unloaded at the large Canton terminal of the Pennsylvania Railroad. *Below,* the Locust Point yards of the Baltimore and Ohio Railroad can handle nearly 3,000 freight cars.

121

N.S. SAVANNAH . . . The world's first nuclear-powered merchant ship visited Baltimore during her trials. She is seen berthed at Dundalk. The sleek 585-foot vessel, which cost about $90,000,000, including development expenses, averages 23 knots but has achieved speeds up to 25 knots. The *Savannah* was built at the Camden, N. J. yard of the New York Shipbuilding Corporation. She is now on display in the city of her name.

CLEARING THE CHANNELS . . . A heavy dredge, its dipper silhouetted, works in the Bay. Channels between Baltimore and the ocean are 42 feet deep and 800 feet wide and provide access for vessels up to 70,000 dead-weight tons. This enables ship traffic to move unencumbered throughout the year to and from Baltimore, with its spacious harbor and 13-inch tidal range.

FOREIGN CARS . . . Baltimore is the largest port in the world for Volkswagen entries. More than 200,000 were expected to pass through the port in 1969, and the ship being unloaded below, at the Dundalk Marine Terminal, carried more than 1,200. Other cars such as MG's and Mercedes Benzes also are imported through Baltimore, and Datsuns and Toyotas, which are manufactured in Japan, recently were added to this list. In mild weather, cars imported through the Baltimore port generally are distributed throughout the eastern states and south through Tennessee. However, when freezing closes the Great Lakes, foreign cars shipped to Baltimore are distributed on a much wider scale, with some going to points as distant as Minnesota, Nebraska and Wisconsin.

GRAIN PIER . . . Baltimore has three massive grain piers which have a total bin capacity exceeding 12,000,000 bushels and a combined loading capability of more than a half million bushels per hour. Adjacent berths, where the water depth varies from 32 to 35 feet, can accommodate ten ships. Above is the Western Maryland Railway pier at Port Covington, with two huge foreign ships being loaded.

PRINCIPAL IMPORT . . . Iron ore, with more than 10,000,-000 tons moving into Baltimore annually, is a principal import and is handled, along with manganese ore and chrome ore, at facilities such as the one at Port Covington, below. Two traveling bridge cranes at this site have an unloading capacity of 2,000 tons per hour, while the total ore unloading capacity at four modern piers with berths for 11 ships is 7,800 tons per hour.

TRANSFER POINT . . . At piers such as this, above, operated by the Western Maryland Railway at Port Covington, incoming cargo is transferred from ships to waiting railroad cars, while general cargo lies in a transit shed to be loaded on the vessels before they depart. The port moves domestic and foreign cargo with speed by utilizing three trunk line railroads, more than 150 motor carriers, eleven airlines and 113 steamship lines that connect it with 270 world ports.

COAL . . . More than 2,500,000 tons of coal and coke are exported through Baltimore annually, much of it passing through this sprawling complex, below, at Port Covington where the Western Maryland Railway has 15 acres of open storage and a rail holding yard for 3,000 cars. Modern equipment gives this pier the capability of loading 3,500 tons per hour, and nearby are three other coal piers that give the port a total loading capacity of almost 10,000 tons per hour.

CRUISES . . . A ship tied up at Baltimore takes on passengers for a cruise to the Caribbean. Such sailings, inaugurated in 1962, carry more than 2,000 persons annually to places like Bermuda, San Juan and St. Thomas in the spring and winter. The ships use Dundalk Marine Terminal.

BANANAS . . . More than 100,000 short tons of bananas are shipped to Baltimore annually for distribution. At a Port Covington pier, below, built by the B&O Railroad to handle banana boats, three gantry cranes 80-feet high and conveyor belts are used to unload an ocean-going vessel.

TOMORROW'S HOUSES . . . Workmen at the Weyerhaeuser pier at Fairfield prepare to unload lumber from a vessel, above, carrying more than 5,500,000 board feet. Much of the lumber shipped to Baltimore comes from Canada, and in 1965 imports totaled about 121,000,000 board feet.

COAL PIER . . . The modern coal loading pier, below, at Curtis Bay is owned and operated by the Baltimore and Ohio-Chesapeake and Ohio railroads. It has four giant electric loading towers and four 60-foot conveyor belts that combine to give it a total loading capacity of 4,800 tons per hour.

"BIG MO" . . . Every June, a task force of battleships, heavy cruisers, escort carriers and destroyer-type vessels moves up the Bay to Annapolis where midshipmen board the ships for the summer cruise. This is the *U.S.S. Missouri,* often flagship of the force. Early in 1950, the 45,000-ton ship spent fifteen ignominious days off Old Point Comfort aground on a Chesapeake Bay mudbank. The battleship, of course, is best known for its role in Tokyo Bay. There, on September 2, 1945, Japanese leaders boarded the ship to sign the instrument of formal surrender to the Allied Power, thus ending World War II.

KENT NARROWS . . . The swirling waters of the narrows, top, separate Kent Island from the mainland of the Eastern Shore and mark the northern juncture of Eastern Bay and the Chesapeake Bay. The area is a center of fishing, oystering and clamming activity.

NANTICOKE . . . On the Nanticoke River near the point where it empties into Tangier Sound, the town of Nanticoke, above, is the national headquarters for a company that processes fish which are frozen and imported from Iceland. Workboats in the picture supply other seafood packing houses.

N.S. ENTERPRISE . . . The world's largest warship and only nuclear-powered aircraft carrier, the *N.S. Enterprise* dwarfs several tugboats as it moves up the James River. The 85,000-ton vessel was built at Newport News shipyard at a cost exceeding $400,000,000. Its electric generating capacity could serve a city of 2,000,000, and from keel to mast the carrier rises 23 stories. Water-cooled nuclear reactors give it the capability of steaming 5 years without refueling. It is 1,040 feet long and 252 feet wide. Among the on-board facilities to serve its company of 3,500 are a hospital and weather bureau. The *Enterprise* and the nuclear-powered ships *Long Beach* and *Bainbridge* sailed around the world in 65 days.

FLIGHT DECK . . . The *Enterprise* was employed in Vietnam where planes were launched against the enemy from the 4.5-acre flight deck, left, and the big carrier won the title "The Floating Hilton" because of its reputation as a good place for servicemen to go for rest and recreation during brief respite from battle.

BRIDGE TUNNEL . . . The 17.5-mile bridge-tunnel across the mouth of the Chesapeake Bay connects the Eastern Shore with the Virginia mainland near Norfolk. The $200,000,000 facility eliminates the last water barrier on the Ocean Highway between New York and Jacksonville, Florida. The two-lane project consists of about thirteen miles of trestle, one and one-half miles of earth-fill causeway, two bridges totalling a mile in length, and two tunnels each more than a mile long. The man-made islands, from which fishing is permitted, anchor the tunnels. A trip across the bridge-tunnel takes about 25 minutes. The ship above is about to pass over one of the tunnels.

THE ISLAND OF JERSEY

TOMATOES, IN CANS AND BASKETS . . . Eastern Shore canneries and packing houses were built along navigable rivers because of cheap water transportation. Today they are busier than ever—their activity can be measured by the "cannery smoke" which drifts for miles across the Shore. But now most of their products are hauled by trucks. *Below*, some Dorchester County tomatoes are still carried to Baltimore by Bay craft.

JERSEY . . . The tiny island of Jersey lies just 26 feet off the tip of Crisfield's Main Street. It is crowded with wharves, seafood packing houses, a marine railway and shops that make oyster tongs and ornate name-boards for sailing vessels, such as the one under the bowsprit of the bugeye *Moonlight*. At least half of the island, about the size of a large baseball park, is composed of oyster shells. The picture of the drawbridge that connects Main Street with Jersey is on page 47.

RECORD BREAKER . . . The *United States* is the largest liner ever built in our country and is hailed as the fastest vessel in the world. Her overall length is 990 feet and her gross tonnage 53,330. The ship, which is powered by steam turbines, carries 2,000 passengers and a crew of 1,000. Work on the design began in March, 1946, and the keel was laid on February 8, 1950. The ship was built by the Newport News Shipbuilding and Dry Dock Company at a cost of $70,000,000. More aluminum was used in the liner than in any other single structure ever built. On her maiden voyage from New York to Le Havre and Southampton in July, 1952, tne United States chopped 10 hours and two minutes off the Queen Mary's trans-Atlantic record of 1938, making the blue ribbon run of 2,942 miles in three days, 10 hours and 40 minutes at an average speed of 35.59 knots. This picture was made at the Norfolk Navy Yard when the ship returned for an overhaul.

HAMPTON ROADS . . . Norfolk, Chesapeake, Newport News and Portsmouth make up Hampton Roads, and the four function as one port unit in one of the world's finest natural harbors. Hampton Roads is the leading coal port of the world and clears about 40,000,000 tons annually. A $25,000,000 coal pier which was opened at Lamberts Point in 1963 has twin traveling loaders, each as high as a 17-story building, that can serve the largest colliers afloat. Some of the colliers have a capacity exceeding 90,000 tons, but the pier has facilities for handling 20,000 tons an hour. At Newport News the Chesapeake and Ohio Railway has an $8,000,000 pier to handle increasing ore imports. At Norfolk is the U.S. Naval Base, largest in the world and home port for much of the Atlantic Fleet. Above is part of the sprawling, modern coal facilities at Lamberts Point.

WORLD TERMINAL . . . Hampton Roads, where more than 5,000 ships sail annually, is the leading Atlantic Coast port in export tonnage and has steamship lines which connect the Virginia ports with practically every major port in the world.

CAR FLOAT . . . This is one of the car floats operated by the Chesapeake and Ohio Railroad on a regular schedule across Hampton Roads. The pilot house rising above the cars sits on steel poles, and when the float is empty the house, from a distance, looks like a gigantic water spider.

TOBACCO . . . Hampton Roads is the largest tobacco port in the world. About 200,000 tons of
Maryland and Virginia tobacco are exported
through it annually to countries such as France,
Switzerland and Germany.

GENERAL CARGO . . . One of more than two doz-
en general cargo piers in the port of Baltimore,
this one is maintained by the Maryland Port Au-
thority. It has berths for five vessels and is served
by four 50-ton gantry cranes.

Resources of the Bay

BEST FISHING HOLE IN AMERICA . . . The Bay, which contains 200 different species of fish, is famous as the best fishing hole in America. Among its best known fish are rock, hardheads, sea trout, Norfolk spot, shad, yellow and white perch, bluefish, black drum, largemouth black bass, blow toads, channel bass, catfish, flounder, sea robin and sharks. Gray trout migrate into the Bay for summer feeding and herring, hickory shad, white shad and menhaden spawn in its waters. Commercial fishermen catch more than 40 species with haul seines, pound, gill, purse and fyke nets. The photograph shows pound fishermen unloading their catch at a packing house.

OYSTER BAY . . . A fleet of Bay craft dredge for oysters, the most valuable of all the Chesapeake's seafood products. In 1964, the last year in which complete figures were available, the Bay yielded 1,340,000 bushels of oysters, valued at more than $4,500,000. The same year watermen harvested more than 25,000,000 pounds of crabs worth almost $3,000,000. The total seafood harvest was 70,000,000 pounds with a value of $12,000,000. About 9,000 Marylanders harvest seafood commercially.

CRAB POUND . . . Crabs kept in these floats have to be watched day and night—hence the electric lights—while they change from hard to soft crabs. During the shedding they are known by the stages they are in—green peeler, peeler, buster, and, finally, soft crab. In keeping his record of the crabs he buys, the pound manager never uses the real name of the crabber, just the nickname. The record book at the Tangier Island pound bears these names: Blue Tail, Pop Corn, Puck, Froggie, Preacher, Whistle, Gutch, Gitt.

WORKING THE BAY . . . With storm clouds blackening the horizon, above, watermen head out to a pound net with their workboat in tow. Below, a sloop and a fleet of skipjacks dredge for oysters over the Rocks off Sharps Island in the Bay. In the center is the sloop *J. T. Leonard* with its top sail furled. Built in 1882, it was the last sloop in commercial service in Bay waters and now is on display at the Chesapeake Bay Maritime Museum in St. Michaels. Despite the general decline of sail in the last 50 years, there are still more commercial sailing craft in the Maryland waters of the Bay than on any other single body of water in our country. This is a result of a Maryland law passed in 1865 which prohibited the use of steam motive power in dredging oysters. The purpose of the act was to conserve the oyster supply. But it also prolonged the use of sailing vessels in the upper Bay where not until 1966 was the use of motive power authorized in dredging, and then only on an experimental basis. Virginia has long permitted motive power in dredging, and commercial sail has disappeared from its waters. In the 1800's there were several thousand commercial sailing vessels on the Bay.

BUGEYE . . . When Maryland repealed a ban on the use of dredges in the 1860's the existing sloops, schooners and pungies were not too well suited for dredging so the bugeye was built to fill the need. It was an enlargement of the brogan, which developed from the log canoe. A bugeye usually has a sharp bow and stern, a centerboard, a jib and "leg-of-mutton" fore and mainsails on sharply raking masts.

SCHOONER . . . The two-masted schooner was once the most popular type of sailing craft on the Bay. It was used for oystering and trading and quite often ventured into the ocean. The *Mattie F. Dean,* shown here, was built in 1884. It was a famous Bay-built schooner and the last of its type to see service on the Chesapeake. A doll-like figure once graced its foremast but is missing in this photograph.

Oyster Dredgers on the Choptank . . . This is the picture that won a five thousand dollar prize in a contest sponsored by *Photography* magazine. It shows the skipjacks Maggie Lee and Lucy Tyler in a driving rain, in which the crew continued to work. They seem oblivious of the weather. Evidence of the intensity of the storm can be found by looking closely at the water, the black spots having been caused by the rain actually knocking holes into the Choptank as it fell. This picture has had a great success in photographic exhibitions at home and abroad, for it has feeling, mood, and dramatic values of high caliber.

MAKING A LICK . . . When a dredge is dragged across an oyster bar by the towing vessel—this is called making a lick—the teeth of the dredge dig into the bar and force the oysters into the bag. When the bag is reasonably full, a donkey engine pulls it up on deck where it is dumped. A properly operated dredge will catch practically every oyster in its path. A vessel uses two dredges at a time.

MENHADEN CENTER . . . Reedville, on the tip of Virginia's Northern Neck, is one of the menhaden centers of the Atlantic Coast. Its fleet roams from the Carolinas to New England in search of menhaden, the most numerous fish in the ocean. Its factories grind up the trash fish for oil, which is used in making such things as soap and linoleum. The residue is used for animal and poultry food.

OYSTER TONGER . . . Hand-tonging for oysters from the slippery deck of a bobbing boat is probably the toughest job there is in the Bay country. The waterman drops his tongs, which resembles two long rakes with facing sets of teeth, to the bottom and then works them back and forth with short strokes to scrape the oysters from their beds. When the tongs are closed the rakes form a basket to hold the catch. The waterman must keep a firm grip on the handles as he pulls up the tongs or the oysters will dribble out of the basket. The catch is dumped on the culling board where the marketable oysters—over three inches in length—are separated from the "illegals" and the shells, which are pushed back. Tongs, of course, become more difficult to operate as the depth of water increases. Most are never used in water over 22 feet deep, but there are some watermen who work with 40-foot handles. Hand tongs are the only device permitted by Maryland law on public oyster beds in most tributaries and in some parts of the Chesapeake Bay.

SEED BED . . . The wide mouth of the James River is the largest and most prolific seed bed for oysters in the Chesapeake Bay area. The spat, the newly set oyster, grows better here than any other place, but, for some strange reason, the oysters never attain much size. The oysters harvested from these rich beds are sold as seed and transplanted in other Virginia waters where they will grow large and fat. The photograph shows a buy boat loading oysters while a fleet of tongers works in the mouth of the James.

HORN HARBOR . . . This busy fishing center, which lies
northeast of Mobjack Bay, is one of the most picturesque
areas of tidewater Virginia. The weathered poles are
known as pound stakes, trap stakes or weir poles.

MENDING THE NETS . . . When the day's fishing is done the watermen stretch their gill nets across poles to check for holes and snags. The men are working on the beach at Betterton, one of the oldest resorts on the Eastern Shore of Maryland.

NET RESULTS . . . Watermen dip a large haul out of the "head," the trap of a pound net. About 20 per cent of the fish taken in the upper waters of the Chesapeake Bay and its tributaries are caught in such nets. The gear is used in water up to 40 feet deep. Some nets are 1,500 feet long.

DRAWING THE PURSE STRINGS . . . Fishermen labor to close their purse net around a school of menhaden in the lower Bay. After a school is spotted from the crow's nest of a mother ship, a striker boat, far right, slips out quietly to mark the school. Two net boats, each about 30-feet long, follow the striker. They make a wide circle around the school, dropping purse seines from the sterns as they go away from each other. The net is about 1,200 feet long and 90 feet wide. When a circle is made the fishermen draw a purse string that closes the net. After the net is pulled in, the bunched fish are dipped out. As many as 500,000 fish have been caught in one net, but not in Maryland where purse netting is illegal. The Menhaden season runs from May until November; the fish are in the Bay during the summer. Menhaden also are called pogy, alewife, oldwife, bunker, mossbunker, bughead, bugfish, and chebog. They are a member of the herring family.

STUDY IN MOTION . . . Five men strain at a haul seine which is heavy with fish. A haul seine, rigged with corks and weights to stand vertically in the water, is dropped around a school of fish then hauled into shallow water near the shore where the catch is removed. Haul seines are effective only when the fish are close to shore. They are usually used to catch croaker, rock, shad and perch.

WORKING THE NETS . . . On a raw October morning watermen prepare to empty a pound net which is a large stationary device of poles and netting arranged to form a trap. A large net with poles costs about $5,500. Pound nets generally are used from March through November.

SNAPPER TRAPPER . . . A Virginia waterman lowers a trap for snapping turtles between two cypress trees on the Chickahominy River. He sells to a packer in Toano, Virginia, who ships 100,000 pounds of snappers, 25,000 pounds of eels and 200,000 pounds of catfish every year. Some catfish weigh 25 pounds.

BOX SCORE . . . Watermen who catch food fish speak of their haul in terms of boxes, and each box always contains 100 pounds. Thus when they say they got "eight boxes" they mean they caught 800 pounds. But fishermen who go after menhaden, the most plentiful fish in the ocean, speak of their haul in terms of millions.

SEAFOOD CAPITAL OF VIRGINIA . . . Hampton, the oldest English community in America, is the seafood capital of Virginia. Its busy fleet of several hundred boats brings in tremendous catches of crabs, oysters and fish. Its venturesome trawlers fish beyond the Capes and often work their way as far north as the New England fishing grounds. This is a view of Hampton Creek.

CRABS . . . The Virginia waterman, left, is crabbing with a patent trotline. When he thinks his baited line is filled with crabs he puts one end of it on the roller attached to the gear. As the boat moves forward the crabs are knocked off the line and through the basket-line funnel into the net. The waterman is shown raising the gear to remove the catch. *Right,* a Maryland crabber in a demasted bateau uses a dip net to get crabs off his trotline. *Below,* a crab steaming shed. Each steamer holds three wire baskets and each basket contains four barrels of crabs. The crabs are steamed seventeen minutes, and then sent to the crabhouse where they are speedily picked.

DISAPPEARING DELICACY . . . Diamondback terrapins, which were enjoyed by Chesapeake gourmets and their guests for generations, today are used mainly as a show-case dish at elaborate dinners. Most of the terrapins, such as those at right, are netted in marshes and stored in a pound. Once worth $4 apiece, terrapins now bring only about $18 a dozen.

ONCE IGNORED . . . For decades men of the Bay looked on soft-shell clams as trash and refused to harvest them. But as oysters became less abundant and other resources dwindled, watermen reappraised the mananose and discovered a "new" industry. Now thousands of bushels of Chesapeake softshells are sold in New England for its clambakes.

CLAMMING . . . Special boats are used for digging soft-shell clams, or mananose, from river bottoms. The clams are dislodged with water jets from a hose and then are pulled up on a conveyor belt for sorting by hand. Soft-shell clams have multiplied rapidly in Bay waters in recent years and some of the best hauls are made in the Miles, Wye, Chester and Choptank rivers. Hard clams, which are harvested on the lower Eastern Shore, are taken in a different manner. Some watermen, occasionally working in hip-deep water, pull them out with rakes. A number of watermen, however, still prefer to dig clams out with their toes. A good foot man can dig 7,000 daily.

INDIAN FISHERMEN . . . Pamunkey Indians gill net for shad during the spring run of the fish on the Pamunkey River. Nearby is West Point which once was called Pamunkee or Paumnkey and served as the chief village of the Paumnkey of the Powhatan Confederacy. Fishing is one of the main sources of income for the dwindling tribe.

SHARK FISHING . . . Sharks ranging from three to five feet in length are snared with gill nets in Great Marchipongo inlet. The sharks are sold as fish food and marketed under the name steakfish or grayfish. Virginia sharks, usually the sand species, have white flaky meat that lacks bones and a fishy flavor.

HOME OF THE MUSKRAT . . . A trapper removes a muskrat from a trap set in front of a muskrat mound-house made
of sticks, mud and grass. From a distance the dwellings,
some of which stand three and four feet high, resemble
weathered haycocks. Muskrats can be trapped only from
January 1 to March 15; their pelts bring about $1.50 apiece
on the local market. Eastern Shoremen consider fried
muskrat—usually called marsh rabbit in restaurants—a real
delicacy. This picture was made on the 11,000-acre Blackwater National Wildlife Refuge, near Cambridge.

CARDBOARD GEESE . . . A flock of high-flying Canada geese ignore the flock of cardboard geese staked out in front of a hunter's pit dug in an Eastern Shore cornfield. Such a pit is legal. Some hunters lure ducks and geese by painting empty beer cans a bright yellow and throwing them near their blinds or pits. From the air the yellow cans look like ears of corn.

SHELL PILES . . . The millions of oyster shells in these mounds along Hampton Creek at Hampton, Virginia, will be used for planting purposes. Both Maryland and Virginia require that packers set aside a certain percentage of their shells for planting on barren grounds. Shells are also ground into grit for poultry feed.

THE BAY TREE . . . Loblolly pine is usually found on the Eastern Shore from the southern half of Maryland on down. It appears in pure stands, as shown here, or mixed with water oak, southern tupelo and wax myrtle. The graceful, fragrant pine, which sometimes reaches a height of 100 feet, is one of the most valuable trees in North America.

TIDEWATER PINE . . . The pulp and paper plant at West Point, Virginia, uses 300,000 cords of tidewater pine every year in making pulp and paper board. West Point was named for the West brothers—three of the four were governors of Virginia. It stands on the peninsula where the Mattaponi and Pamunkey rivers unite to form the York River.

ACKNOWLEDGEMENTS

When a book of this type is completed, one pauses and reflects how utterly impossible it would have been without the aid of countless friends and numerous business acquaintances. To them, I am eternally grateful. I would like to mention a few who were most directly responsible for the fulfillment of my desire to see a compact story of the great Chesapeake Bay.

First, to Stanley L. Cahn, who organized and followed through in producing the project, my deep thanks. He is the first to acknowledge the artistic assistance of the Caldwells, father, J. Albert, and son, John A., who again did such a superb job of printing this volume. Their craftsmen at Universal Lithographers have now won two national awards for the quality of lithography in Bodine documentaries.

Also, my deep appreciation to Harold A. Williams for the preparation of text and editorial work and especially for his masterful summarization of the Bay. Revisions in this edition are the devoted work of Malcolm M. Allen, a co-worker on *The Sunday Sun* with a wide knowledge of the subject.

To Robert Burgess, of the Mariners' Museum, who acted as guide and companion on some of the expeditions.

To the *Baltimore Sun* for permission to use many of the photographs appearing in the *Sunday Sun Magazine*.

To the Virginia Fisheries Laboratory at Gloucester Point, to the Maryland Biological Research Laboratory at Solomons Island, the Maryland Tidewater Fisheries and the Virginia State Fisheries and to the great services of the government—Army, Navy, Coast Guard, Air Force, and the U. S. Fish and Wildlife Service.

Finally, thanks to the many gracious boat captains who so kindly piloted me through the Bay, and the countless rivers, creeks, and coves, searching for scenes of beauty.

A. A. B.

JOURNEY'S END . . . The sister tidewater states, Maryland and Virginia, both appear in this photograph. Virginia is beyond Port Tobacco Creek and the Potomac River. The picture was made at Chapel Point, Maryland, from the cemetery.

INDEX